ANCIENT MYSTERIES OF THE BIBLE REVEALED

ANCIENT MYSTERIES OF THE BIBLE REVEALED

Vernon Sayers

Copyright © 2007 by Vernon Sayers

ANCIENT MYSTERIES OF THE BIBLE REVEALED
by Vernon Sayers

Printed in the United States of America

ISBN 978-1-60034-934-8

All rights reserved solely by the author. The author guarantees all contents are original and do not infringe upon the legal rights of any other person or work. No part of this publication may be reproduced, stored in a retrieval system, or transmitted in any form or by any means; for example, electronic, photocopy, recording without the prior written permission of the author. The only exception is brief quotations in printed reviews. The views expressed in this book are not necessarily those of the publisher.

Unless otherwise indicated, Bible quotations taken from Old Testament scriptures will be taken from the Tanakh, or the New Jewish Bible, copyright © 1985; the New JPS, copyright © 1985 or Jewish Publication Society Version, copyright © 1985. New Testament scriptures will be taken from the King James Version of the Bible.

www.xulonpress.com

v

This book is dedicated to Isabelle Carvalho Sayers:
Reverend, Mother, Grandmother, and Great-Grandmother,
whose traditional Christian values made this entire book possible,
and to the faithful Holy Spirit who came into my heart
and life because of her.

Table of Contents

Introduction.. xiii

Testimonial xv

Chapter 1 - The Father: The "Only" True God 21

   1. What does God look like?...21
   2. What does the Bible mean when it says that we are made in the image of God?...27
   3. What is God's glory? 29
   4. Does the Bible say anything else concerning God's physical appearance? 30

Chapter 2 - The Day of the LORD..33

   1. What is the sword of God? And what are His arrows?......33
   2. Will God Himself return to earth at the same time as Jesus Christ? And what is that day called in the Bible?.............34
   3. When will the Day of the LORD take place? 37
   4. What will the Day of the LORD be like? 40

Chapter 3 - The Work of the Holy Spirit......................................57

   1. What is a spirit? What is the difference between spirits and the Holy Spirit? And does man really have three parts — body, soul, and spirit? 57
   2. What does the Holy Spirit look like? And what is his assignment from God?..60
   3. What part does the Holy Spirit have in God's plan of salvation? 62

ANCIENT MYSTERIES OF THE BIBLE REVEALED

Chapter 4 - The Lamb of God: Our Elder Brother..........................65

    1. If there is only *one* God, who is Jesus Christ? And what makes him different from Mohammed, Buddha, and Confucius? 65

    2. What is the biblical millennium? And what will this millennium be like before, during, and at the end?....................70

    3. What is the resurrection of the dead? What kind of body will a person receive at the resurrection? And how many resurrections will there be? 73

Chapter 5 - Israel: The Children of God 77

    1. Who was Abraham? And what was the covenant that God made with him and his descendents? 77

    2. What is the Real name of God's children, Christian or Israel?..79

    3. What is a saint? And what does someone have to do to become one?..83

Chapter 6 - Heaven: The Tabernacle of God 85

    1. How many heavens are there? Where is the Real Heaven? And what are the different names for Heaven?.................85

    2. How did God create heaven and earth? And what is the difference between the light and darkness in Genesis 1:1-5, and the lights of the sun, moon, and stars in Genesis 1:14?...87

    3. What does Heaven look like? 89

Chapter 7 - The Lake of Fire: Eternal Chastisement 93

    1. What is the difference between hell and the lake of fire? Where are hell and the lake of fire located? And why did God choose fire as an eternal punishment?......................93

ANCIENT MYSTERIES OF THE BIBLE REVEALED

Chapter 8 - Satan..97

  1. Who is Satan? What does he look like? And how did
     he fall from his position in Heaven?.............................97
  2. What kind of power does Satan use against mankind?
     And where is he now?..99
  3. Is there a difference between the man of sin and the
     Antichrist? What is the ethnicity of the Antichrist? And
     how is Satan involved? 101

Chapter 9 - Angels, Cherubs, and Seraphs....................103

  1. What are angels? How many different kinds are there?
     What do they look like? And how powerful are they?.....103
  2. What are cherubs? How many are there? And what do
     they look like?...106
  3. What are seraphs? How many are there? And what do they
     look like? 108

Introduction

Ever since God first revealed Himself to humanity on Mount Sinai, and ever since its conception, Judeo-Christianity has always believed in one God. However, while Judaism speaks of only one God, its Christianity counter-part speaks of this same God showing Himself in three persons: The Father, the Son, and the Holy Spirit.

For 2,000 years, this doctrinal teaching of Christianity, commonly known as the "Trinity" has created a wall of separation between both faiths, causing debates among Church leaders and Jewish scholars from all over the world, and though many have tried to decipher this mystery and to make sense of it, none has been able to give us a clear answer. However, I believe that mysteries are meant to be solved and old walls are meant to be broken down.

In *Ancient Mysteries of the Bible Revealed* this wall between Judaism and Christianity is about to come down. In this book, you will discover the Identity of the one and only true God of ancient Israel. In addition, you will also learn the difference between the God of Israel and the position that Jesus Christ and the Holy Spirits have in the Godhead. Moreover, you will also discover other ancient secrets that was previously hidden from the understanding of humanity for centuries, all based on the identity of God Himself.

This book will take advantage of the Tanakh for the Old Testament. For its clarity in revealing the true meaning of the ancient Hebrew words themselves, as well as the traditional King James Version for the New Testament. In addition, although the Tanakh is used for the Old Testament, the traditional King James can be used to read the Old Testament references as well.

This book was designed to be read along with the Bible, and as such was not designed to entertain. Instead, it was written to address the subject that has been misunderstood by so many throughout the centuries. The identity of the one God of Judeo-Christianity is finely revealed!

May the answers in this book deepen your faith and understanding of God and may they make your walk with God even more adventurous. God bless you!

Vernon Sayers
Redmond, OR

Testimonial

My name is Vernon Sayers, and I would like to share my testimony, as well as my knowledge of the LORD with you. Like many people I was raised in a Christian environment. My grandmother was a reverend of a small Pentecostal church of twelve that was called "God Our Refuge and Strength Full Gospel Mission."

From childhood, I have always felt God's hand on my life, but I have never really understood why until now. Like many others, I have studied the Bible for years, but unlike scholars and theologians, as well as those who have gone to Bible collage to learn the scriptures, I have been very blessed since a young age to have a very good understanding of the things of God. Some of my understanding came from my grandmother, who taught me the basics of salvation, like being born again, being led of the Holy Spirit, keeping oneself pure from the ways of the world, and so forth. However, the majority of my knowledge concerning the deep things of God was a special gift that I received from the LORD after I became born again. In 1990 at the age of 16, I went to visit my grandmother who was in the hospital having major surgery. After saying goodbye to my grandmother for the day, I went home to watch a television program about Jesus in his early years, when he was a young child. I remember having the desire to open and read my Bible that was laying right next to me on a little table that I had in my bedroom, and as soon as I opened it, I came across the scriptures concerning the unpardonable sin. Now at this time I was not a born-again Christian, and after I read that verse, for some strange reason I started to feel very afraid and very lonely, because I wondered if it was possible for anyone in the world, including myself, to commit such a sin. I sat and worried about this for a while, and eventually evil thoughts concerning that verse started to come into my mind and torment me. After a while, I literally felt a very cold feeling come over me, as if a block of ice was being packed inside of my chest. My mind raced with desperate questions: *Did I commit this sin? Why are these thoughts coming into my mind and tormenting me?*

Two months prior to this incident, my mother, and my step-dad were thinking of finding another apartment for us, but the property owner who my parents were renting from did not want us to leave. However, soon after this incident occurred, he told us that he wanted us to move out. To this day, I do not think that was a coincidence. After moving out, I spent two full years tormented in my mind concerning the unpardonable sin. No matter what I did, no matter how much I prayed, I felt so separated from God that I literally felt like I had no hope; I literally felt like I was already in hell. Upon reaching my 18th birthday, I was lying down on my bed, sometime in the afternoon, and after two years of asking God for His forgiveness and not receiving an answer, I became a little skeptical, and I remember saying to myself, "Maybe this is all in my head." Then moments later, I remember saying these words in a soft voice, "Jesus, save me!" As soon as I said that, what I had experienced that day can never be explained to me by anyone that I have ever met. I know what it's like to feel electricity go through my body, because I accidentally got shocked from an electric outlet a few times as a child. Moreover, I know what it's like to experience the feelings of cold, heat, a breezy wind passing over my body, pins and needles, and goose bumps. However, as soon as I said those words, "Jesus, save me!" I literally felt what was like an invisible human body being lowered from the ceiling of my bedroom into my body. I felt the head, the shoulders, the arms, the legs, and the feet, the entire body, though solid and round or shapely like a real human body, pass right through me, but at the same time, still felt solid. Upon entering my body, the tormented thoughts that had plagued me for those two years left me. A big smile came over my face, and I was filled with overwhelming joy.

At that moment, I knew that I had never committed that sin as I thought I did, but I now realize that what was actually happening to me during those two years was that Satan was holding me in bondage, and he was trying to convince me that I did commit it, and he used that as a way to torment me. Since then, I do not know why God chose to reveal Himself that way to me, because I felt that above all people I didn't deserve to experience that. But I know that I was very privileged to have this experience, because in the fifteen years of being a Christian that have passed since, I have never heard of anyone else having the same experience. Beyond that experience that I had with the LORD, I noticed that as soon as I became born-again, I was able to memorize scriptures and understand them better, whereas before that I could not remember most of the verses that I read, let alone understand them.

After the passing of my grandmother in 1997, like most people after losing a loved one, I have often found myself struggling with my faith. Although I cannot deny what I experienced that day in my bedroom, I can honestly say that had it not been for that experience, and had the LORD not delivered me from the tormented thoughts that I had for those two years. I'm not sure if I would still be a Christian today, because that experience is what keeps me going. Many people have often asked me, "If you know so much concerning the Bible, why do you struggle with your faith?" The answer that I give them is that I'm reminded of the prophet Elijah. Here was a man that experienced things and saw things that most of us may never get to see in our lifetime. The Bible says that he called fire down from heaven; he was visited by an angel of God who came to him and gave him bread for his journey to Mount Horeb; he prayed that it would not rain for three years and six months and it did not. However, despite all the things that he saw with his own eyes, and despite all the things that he experienced with the LORD. The Bible says that he became so depressed after Jezebel, the wife of King Ahab threatened him, that he ran away and wanted the LORD to take his life (James 5:17, 1 Kings 18:18-39, and 1 Kings 19:1-8). I believe the reason why many Christians, including myself, find ourselves oftentimes struggling with our faith, is because we are only human, and we tend to forget the things that we have experienced, and we look more at our circumstances rather than the things we know to be true.

Many years after my grandmother passed away, I noticed that I was being led of the LORD more into the Old Testament, and it was around that time that I started to receive visions of the LORD and His return. I have always asked the LORD many times, "Why me?" "Why are you revealing these things to me?" Surly there are others more deserving than me to receive these revelations, because I didn't have much of an audience in the first place to hear me, and at the same time, I knew that it couldn't be just for my own benefit. I'm not a pastor, I'm not a great speaker, and I feel nervous just by being in a large crowd. Therefore, I didn't know why God was choosing to reveal these things to me, someone who had never gone to a Bible college or studied the scriptures for many years like theologians and scholars. Though I do not consider myself a prophet by calling or vocation, I do know that according to Amos 3:7 the LORD only reveals His secretes to His servants the prophets. So I guess I might be one.

The book you hold in your hand contains answers to questions that have been a mystery to humanity and believers for centuries, answers which I believe God has given me to share with you. Whether you are Jewish, Christian, or Muslim, if you have ever asked yourself questions such as, "What does God look like?" "Who is Jesus Christ?" "Who will the Anti-Christ be?" "What do angels look like?" "Will there really be a rapture of the church?" "When will Jesus Christ return?" "What will the day of the LORD be like?" "How did God create heaven and earth?" and "What does Heaven look like?" The answers to these questions and much more will finally be revealed to you. I have written this book in a question-and-answer format, and when quoting scripture references, I have placed emphasis on particular words to emphasize the true meaning of the words themselves, in order for you to better understand them. The answers from this book come directly from the Bible. I believe the Bible is the inspired Word of God. Many have often said that men wrote the Bible, and though that is partly true, God moved upon these men and gave them the words to write. Have you ever wondered why those who say, "I don't believe the Bible because it was written by men, so therefore I don't read it," are the same ones you see picking up and reading other books *that were written by men*? I believe the reason why many do not read the Bible is that they innately know that reading the Bible will change their lives. The power that it has in transforming the human soul is one of the reasons why I believe the Bible is the inspired Word of God.

I have a saying: "In order to really understand the things of God, you must first know what He looks like; after that, everything else will fall into place." This is the reason why the first chapter of this book focuses on God's physical appearance. It is my prayer for you that as you read this book you will come to an understanding of who God truly is, what He looks like, what He really wants for your life, and how important you really are to Him.

Vernon Sayers
Redmond, OR

Chapter 1

The Father: The "Only" True God

1. What does God look like?

There are many mysteries in the world, but none of them has plagued humanity as much as this particular one, because ever since the beginning of time man has often asked himself, "If there is a God, what does He look like?" This question has also been a mystery to theologians and believers for centuries, despite the fact that many of them are still content with saying that Jesus Christ is the only physical representation of God. And ever since the birth of Christ, theologians, believers, and even non-believers alike have accepted that as true.

But is it really the truth? Because if you were living during the time of Moses, and you were to ask him or anyone that was there, who did you see on Mount Sinai? Most likely Jesus Christ would not be the words that would have come out of their mouth. Because according to the Bible there is only "One" God and this "One" God is only known as the Father. The Bible says that God, who is the Father of all creation, is a visible Spirit, and He also has a physical appearance that is quite different from that of Jesus Christ.

I'm not referring to His facial appearance, because it clearly says in *Exodus 33:20*, "You cannot see My face, for man may not see Me and live." I'm referring to Him physically, the way He revealed Himself to Moses and the ancient Israelites on Mount Sinai as the

God of Israel. Throughout history, the answer from many theologians was that God is invisible and that He fills both the heavens and the earth, or that God only reveals Himself in the person of Jesus Christ. However, according to the Bible, these answers are partly right and partly wrong. The Bible does say in Colossians 1:15 that God is invisible, but it also says that throughout history He chooses to hide Himself and that He only reveals Himself physically during major world events. This means that He is visible, but He chooses to be invisible, as it says in *Isaiah 45:15*: "You are indeed a God who concealed Himself, O God of Israel, who bring victory!"

God does fill both heaven and earth, according to Jeremiah 23:24, but it's not because He has no shape or form, but rather it's because He fills heaven and earth through His Spirit, who represents Him, that occupies every living creature in both heaven and earth. For example, if you consider that the life force or the breath of life in man, or in any other living creature for that matter, like animals, birds, fish, and so forth, that causes us to be living creatures or beings, with the ability to move about, think, choose, and feel, is the Spirit of God. Who is literally a [part] of God or in other words, His child or His offspring (Numbers 16:22, Numbers 27:16, Malachi 2:10, 1 Corinthians 15:39, and Genesis 7:21-22). Then because it is His Spirit in you and me, as well as in any other creature, He automatically knows where we are, what we are doing, what we are looking at, what we are hearing, and what comes into our minds. As it says in *Psalms 139:7-10*, "Where can I escape from Your Spirit? Where can I flee from Your presence? If I ascend to heaven, You are there; If I descend to sheol, You are there too. If I take wing with the dawn to come to rest on the western horizon, even there Your hand will be guiding me, Your right hand will be holding me fast."

That is the reason why Jesus himself said in the gospel of Matthew 10:29, that when a bird falls to the ground, God automatically knows about it. Because it was His breath of life or His Spirit that was in the bird that caused it to be a living creature. Therefore, God sees and knows everything that His Spirit sees and knows, because His Spirit is a part of Him. This is not to be confused with the teachings of those in the new age movement who say that God's breath of life or His Spirit is also in the trees or in the rocks or in a nail; the Bible does not teach that. Though it is possible for God to give life to inanimate objects like rocks or stones if He wanted to (Matthew 3:9 and Luke 19:40). Because we must remember that when God made man from the dust of the ground, man was literally an inanimate object himself, an empty shell, until God's breath of life or His Spirit went into his lifeless body through his nose and made him a living being, soul, or creature (Genesis 2:7). However, I must also point out that this does not mean that an atheist is a child of God just because he has the Spirit of God inside of him. He is in a sense a child of God, because his spirit, who makes up the real him did come from God. But the Bible tells us that every man that is born into this world becomes separated from God at birth because of sin. Moreover, according to John 1:12, we do not have the power or the right to be called the sons and daughters of God again until we accept Jesus Christ as our Lord and Savior, who was sent by God to redeem us back to Himself (John 17:1-3).

God does reveal Himself in the person of Jesus Christ, but in terms of his physical appearance, Jesus Christ is the only begotten "Son" of God, not God Himself. A good example of this is where Jesus reveals to the rich man the difference between himself and God in *Mark 10:17-18*: "And when he was gone forth into the way, there came one running, and kneeled to him, and asked him, Good Master, what shall I do that I may inherit eternal life? And Jesus said unto him, 'Why callest thou *me* good? There is none good but *one*, that is God.'"

As you can see from this verse, Jesus is making a clear distinction between himself and God when he says that there is none good but *one* and that is God Himself, who is only known as the Father. Another example is in John 14:1: "Let not your heart be troubled: ye believe in God, believe *also* in me."

There are also these examples placed back to back, starting with the gospel of *John 4:24*: God is a *Spirit:* and they that worship Him must worship Him in spirit and in truth." *Luke 24:39*: "Behold my hands and my feet, that it is I myself: handle me, and see; for a [spirit] "hath not" flesh and bones, as ye see me have." *Hosea 11:9*: "I will not act on My wrath, I will not turn to destroy Ephraim. For I am God, *not* man, the Holy One in your midst: I will not come in fury."

There are those who say that God does not have a physical appearance, and they say this based on what Jesus said to the apostle Philip in *John 14:8-9*: "Philip saith unto him, 'Lord, show us the Father, and it sufficeth us.' Jesus saith unto him, 'Have I been so long time with you, and yet hast thou not known me, Philip? He that hath seen me hath seen the Father; and how sayest thou then, Show us the Father?'"

I believe what Jesus is referring to here is the Spirit of God, who represents the Father inside of him who is doing the works or revealing to us the Father's ways and personality. Because notice what he says in the next verse, in verse 10: "Believest thou not that I am *in* the Father, and the Father *in* me? The words that I speak unto you I speak not of myself: but the Father that dwelleth *in* me, he doeth the works." Another example of why many believe that God does not have a physical appearance is found in *1 John 4:12:* "No man hath seen God at any time. If we love one another, God dwelleth in us, and His love is perfected in us."

Here again, we must go back to Exodus 33:20 where it says that no man can see His *face* and live. A few places in the Bible seem to spell the word God with a capital G, which means the Father or God Himself, next to the word Jesus Christ. However, according to the Bible, we must remember that Jesus Christ is the [mediator] *between* God and man. As it says in 1 Timothy 2:5: "For there is *one* God, and *one* [mediator] *between* God and men, the *man* Christ Jesus ..." So because he represents both sides, he is often referred to as the *Son* of man, to *represent* man, and he is often referred to as the Lord *God*, to *represent* God.

Throughout the gospels, Jesus makes many references to the difference between himself and God. Another one of them is found in John 20:17: "Jesus saith unto her, touch me not; for I am not yet ascended to my Father: but go to my *brethren,* and say unto them, I ascend unto *my* Father and *your* Father; and to *my* God and your God. So if Jesus is God Himself, he would not be able to say *My* Father and *your* Father; and to *My* God, and *your* God.

Moreover, there are also those who say, "Didn't Jesus say in John 10:30 that 'I and my Father are one'?" "And didn't he also say to the Jews in *John 8:58,* 'before Abraham was, I am'?" Yes he did.

However, I believe what Jesus meant when he said that he is *one* with the Father, was that he is *one* with Him in spirit and in right standing with Him. At that time, no one else could say that, because no one else was *one* with the Father in spirit and in right standing with Him, because we were separated from the Father since birth because of our sin. Notice what he says here concerning us in *John 17:21*: "That *they* all may be [one]; as thou, Father, [art *in* me] and [I *in* thee], that *they* also may be [one *in* us]: that the world may believe that thou hast sent me.

As for saying to the Jews in *John 8:58*, "Before Abraham was, I am," we are told that the spirit of Jesus Christ was once *inside* of God and *came out* of God, just like all other spirits (John 8:42, John 16:27, and John 17:8). The Bible says that before the creation of the world, the spirit of Christ was the *first* Holy Spirit to be born of God or to come out of God (Colossians 1:15). Jesus abided with God until the set time, when he was to be sent to earth by God to be born of a virgin woman. As it says here concerning where he was after coming out of the Father before the world was created, as well as how he represents the Father in terms of salvation by bearing His (name) in *Micah 5:1-3*: "And you, O Bethlehem of Ephrath, least among the clans of Judah, from you [one] shall come forth to rule Israel [for Me]-one whose *origin* is from of old, [from ancient times]. Truly, God will leave Israel [helpless] *until* [she] who is to bear has borne; then the rest of *his* country men shall return to the children of Israel. *He* shall stand and shepherd by the *might* of the LORD, by the power of the *name* of the LORD *his* God, and they shall dwell [secure]. For lo, *he* shall wax great to the ends of the earth."

This is the reason why the Bible tells us in John 1:1 that in the [beginning] or just *before* God created heaven and earth, Jesus (the Word) was *with* God, and he *was* God, because as a Holy Spirit he represented God. In addition, because he is God's anointed and chosen one to redeem humanity back to Himself, he still bears the Father's *name* to represent Him for the sake of salvation. Just like how we sometimes bear our parent's last name, but in reality we are not our parents.

The Bible gives us a clue as to God's physical appearance in *Isaiah 33:14-15*: "Sinners in Zion are frightened, the godless are seized with trembling: 'Who of us can dwell with the devouring fire: who of us can dwell with the never-dying blaze?' He who walks in righteousness, speaks uprightly, spurns profit from fraudulent dealings, waves away a bribe instead of grasping it, stops his ears against listening to infamy, shuts his eyes against looking at evil."

Clearly, this verse is not implying that if we do well spiritually then we get to dwell with eternal hell-fire. According to the Bible, the first recorded account of God's physical appearance is in Exodus 19. Here, God reveals Himself to Moses and the ancient Israelites on Mount Sinai as a massive and visible Spirit of everlasting devouring fire. In Exodus 19:9-11 and 16-22, Moses describes what they saw:

And the LORD said to Moses, "I will come to you in a thick cloud, in order that the people may hear when I speak with you and so trust you ever after." Then Moses reported the people's words to the LORD, and the LORD said to Moses, "Go to the people and warn them to stay pure today and tomorrow. (Let them wash their clothes). Let them be ready for the third day; for on the third day [the LORD will come down, in the sight of all the people, on Mount Sinai].

On the third day, as morning dawned, there was thunder, and lightning, and a dense cloud upon the mountain, and a very loud blast of the horn; and all the people who were in the camp trembled. Moses led the people out of the camp [toward God], and they took their places at the foot of the mountain. Now Mount Sinai was all in smoke, for [the LORD] had come down upon it [in fire]; the smoke rose like the smoke of a kiln, and all the people trembled violently. The blare of the horn grew louder and louder. As Moses spoke, God answered him in thunder. The LORD came down upon Mount Sinai, on the top of the mountain, and the LORD called Moses to the top of the mountain and Moses went up. The LORD said to Moses, "Go down, warn the people not to break through to the LORD to gaze, lest many of them perish. The priest also, who come near the LORD, "must" stay pure, lest [the LORD] "break out" against them."

The Bible says that God is Holy and that no unclean thing can stand in His presence. For many years, theologians have said that evil cannot exist in His presence, because there is so much love that comes out of God that darkness or evil cannot exist in His presence at the same time. However, as we have just read, this is not about His love at all, but it concerns His fire. In Exodus 19:21-22, the Bible says that this is something automatic, and something that He cannot prevent when He is *physically* present. This explains why God warns Moses (twice), not to let any unclean person pass the boundaries of the mountain to gaze at the LORD. Because any creature that comes too close to Him, man or beast, that is not clean physically and spiritually, would not be able to survive in His presence, because according to Exodus 19:9-22, God is literally a massive and visible Spirit of everlasting consuming fire, and His fire would automatically "break out" against them and destroy them!

2. What does the Bible mean when it says that we are made in the image of God?

Ever since God first revealed Himself to Moses and the ancient Israelites on Mount Sinai as a devouring fire, He has often revealed His physical appearance to His servants the prophets through visions and dreams. One of these prophets was Ezekiel. In his vision, Ezekiel saw a very detailed image of God that was not revealed to his ancestors.

According to the writings of Moses in the books of Exodus and Deuteronomy, when God first revealed Himself to Moses and the ancient Israelites, they saw a pavement under Him that was made of sapphire, clear blue as the sky itself. However, they did not see a throne, and they did not see anyone or anything in the fire; they only heard the sound of the thunderous words that were emanating from it. As it says here, starting with *Exodus 24:9-11:* "Then Moses and Aaron, Nadab and Abihu, and seventy elders of Israel ascended; and [they saw the God of Israel]: under His feet there was the likeness of a pavement of sapphire, like the very [sky] for purity. Yet He did not raise His hand against the leaders of the Israelites; [they beheld God], and they ate and drank."

ANCIENT MYSTERIES OF THE BIBLE REVEALED

Deuteronomy 4:9-12, 15-19, 24, 33, 36: But take utmost care and watch yourselves scrupulously, so that you [do not forget the things that you saw with your own eyes] and so that they do not fade from your mind as long as you live. And make them known to your children and to your children's children: the day you stood before the LORD your God at Horeb, when the LORD said to me, "Gather the people to Me that I may let them hear My words, in order that they may learn to revere Me as long as they live on earth, and may so teach their children.' You came forward and stood at the foot of the mountain. The mountain was ablaze with flames to the very skies, dark with densest clouds. [The LORD spoke to you out of the fire]; you heard the sound of words [but perceived no shape-nothing but a voice]. For your own sake, therefore, be most careful — since you saw no shape when the LORD your God spoke to you at Horeb out of the fire — not to act wickedly and make for yourselves a sculptured image in any likeness whatever: the form of a man or a woman, the form of any beast on earth, the form of any winged bird that flies in the sky, the form of anything that creeps on the ground, the form of any fish that is in the waters below the earth. And when you look up to the sky and behold the sun and the moon and the stars, the whole heavenly host, you must not be lured into bowing down to them or serving them. These the LORD your God allotted to other peoples everywhere under heaven. For the LORD your God is a consuming fire, an impassioned God. Has any people heard the voice of a god speaking out of a fire, as you have, and survived? From the heavens He let you hear His voice to discipline you; on earth [He let you see His great fire]; and from amidst that fire you heard His words.

When God first revealed Himself to the ancients, He did so with caution. Because when God first made man, He made him in His own image or likeness, which means that God does have the shape or form of a human being, just as Jesus said concerning God having a shape in *John 5:37.* However, He did not allow them to see His true image, because He knew their hearts. He knew that as soon as He would allow them to see His true likeness, their hearts would be tempted to make a sculptured image of Him. Therefore, we find that God intentionally covered Himself with His fire so that the people would not go astray. His true likeness is revealed starting with Ezekiel.

Ezekiel 1:26-28: Above the expanse over their heads was the semblance of a throne, in appearance like sapphire; and on top, upon this semblance of a throne, there was the semblance of a [human form]. From what appeared as His loins up, I saw a gleam as of amber — what looked like [a fire "encased" in a frame]; and from what appeared as His loins down, I saw what looked like fire. There was a radiance all about Him. Like the appearance of the bow which shines in the clouds on a day of rain, such was the appearance of the surrounding radiance. That was the appearance of the semblance of the Presence of the LORD.

Ezekiel 8:1-3: In the sixth year, on the fifth day of the sixth month, I was sitting at home, and the elders of Judah were sitting before me, and there the "hand" of the Lord God fell upon me. As I looked, there was a figure that had the appearance of fire: from what appeared as His loins down, [He was] fire; and from His loins up, His appearance was resplendent and had the "color" of amber. He stretched out the [form of a hand], and took me by the hair of my head.

So according to the Bible, God is a massive and visible Spirit of immense everlasting fire in the [shape] of a human being. And His rainbow that is spoken of in Genesis 9:12-17, that is stretched out in the sky on a rainy day, can be seen radiating all around His throne, and His throne is made out of a massive sky blue sapphire stone. Therefore, the words in Genesis 1:26 are now better to understand. And God said, "Let us make man in our image, after our likeness."

3. What is God's glory?

Many theologians have tried to answer this question by saying that God's glory is the brilliant white light that shines out of His face and body, and this is true when it comes to the Lord Jesus Christ, the angels, and for those resurrected from the dead when he returns with God, according to Daniel 12:2-3. However, when it comes to God, His glory is His body of fire, as it says here in *Revelation 15:8:*

And the Temple was filled with [smoke] from the "glory" of God, and from His power; and no man was able to enter into the Temple till the seven plagues of the seven angels were fulfilled.

4. Does the Bible say anything else concerning God's physical appearance?

Yes. He has a robe that envelopes or covers His glory or His body of fire that is made out of light itself, and it gives off rays of light in every direction, and these rays are referred to as the skirts of His robe. Its color is white like snow, and His hair is like lambs wool, as it says here, starting with *Psalms 104:1-2*: Bless the LORD, O my soul; O LORD, my God, You are very great; You are clothed in glory and majesty, wrapped in a [robe of light]; You spread the heavens like a tenth cloth. *Isaiah 6:1*: In the year that King Uzziah died, I beheld my Lord seated on a high and lofty throne; and [the skirts of His robe filled the Temple]. *Habakkuk 3:4:* It is a brilliant light which gives off rays on every side-and therein [His glory is enveloped]. *Daniel 7:9*: As I looked on, Thrones were set in place, and the Ancient of Days took His seat. [His garment was like white snow, and the hair of His head was like lamb's wool].

He appears to have the "color" of a Jasper or a Sardine stone, which usually has the color of amber, because He is fire, and His rainbow that is spoken of in Genesis 9:12-17 and Ezekiel 1:28, is [bent around] His throne into the "shape" of an Emerald, as it says here in *Revelation 4:3*: And He that sat was to look upon like a Jasper and a Sardine stone: and there was [a rainbow] "round about" the throne, in sight like unto an Emerald.

And just as in ancient kings' palaces, there was a long red carpet placed underneath their throne and then extending outward for those approaching their throne, God has one too, but His is made entirely out of water that sparkles like crystal. In addition, it contracts to a confined space or area underneath His throne that takes the form of a pavement of floating water for His throne to rest upon when He travels through the heavens. Moreover, it rolls out like a carpet to form a river when He is in Heaven, as it says here, starting with

Ezekiel 1:22: Above the heads of the creatures was [a form]: [an expanse], with an awe-inspiring [gleam as of crystal, was spread out above their heads]. *Revelation 22:1:* And he showed me [a pure river of water of life, clear as crystal, proceeding out] of the throne of God and of the Lamb.

Moreover, the Bible does not give us an exact measurement, but it gives us a clue as to how tall He may actually be in Exodus 33:21-23. And the LORD said, "See, there is a place near Me. Station yourself on the rock and, as My Presence passes by, I will put you in a cleft of the rock and shield you with My hand until I have passed by. Then I will take My hand away and you will see My back; but [My face must not be seen]."

If you noticed what it said here concerning His hand, if His hand was large enough to shield the entire view of Moses, so that Moses couldn't see Him, there is a strong possibility that His height may exceed fifteen feet.

Chapter 2

The Day of the LORD

1. What is the sword of God? And what are His arrows?

In the Bible, whenever there's a reference to God's physical sword and arrows, it always refers to His fire and lightning. This is not to be confused with verses in scripture that says His Word is His sword, or where it says "your arrows stick fast in me" as in Psalms 38:2-3. In the Bible, whenever God's fire or sword comes out of Him to consume anything, most of the time it comes out of His mouth, as it says here, starting with Isaiah 30:27. Behold the LORD Himself comes from afar in blazing wrath, with a heavy burden — His lips full of fury, His tongue like devouring fire. *Isaiah 66:16:* For [with fire] will the LORD contend, [with His sword], against all flesh; and many shall be the slain of the LORD. *Psalms 18:9*: Smoke went up from His nostrils, [from His mouth came devouring fire]; live coals blazed forth from Him.

Whenever lightning comes out of God, the Bible says that it comes out of His hands and arms, in a display of His power, as it says here, starting with *Job 36:32*: Lightning fills His hands; He orders it to hit the mark. *Psalms 144:6:* Make lightning flash and scatter them; shoot your arrows and rout them. *Zechariah 9:14*: And the LORD will manifest Himself to them, and His arrows shall flash like lightning. *Isaiah 30:30*: For the LORD will make His majestic voice heard and display the sweep of [His arm] in raging wrath, in a devouring blaze of fire, in tempest, and rainstorm, and hailstones.

2. Will God Himself return to earth at the same time as Jesus Christ? And what is that day called in the Bible?

Yes, God Himself will return to earth at the same time as Jesus Christ. Today there are many in the church who believe in a theory called the rapture of the church, where our Lord Jesus Christ will come back to earth in secret before his second coming to resurrect his followers from the dead and to snatch away his people like a thief. In addition, many believe in this secret rapture theory because of what the Bible says here in *1 Thessalonians 5:2*: For yourselves know perfectly that the day of the Lord so cometh as a thief in the night.

So because of this verse and others, like Luke 21:28-36 and 1 Thessalonians 1:10, many interpret these scriptures to mean a secret catching away, where we will "escape" and be "delivered" from the wrath to come. However, I believe what the Lord is referring to here by the word "escape" in Luke 21:36 and the word "delivered" in 1 Thessalonians 1:10, is to flee, evade, and avoid. This alludes to how we will be kept safe during all the chaos and wrath that will come upon the entire world if we separate ourselves from the lifestyle the world is taking; thus "The Day of the LORD" will not come upon "us" unawares like a thief as it will the rest of the world. As it says here, starting with *1 Thessalonians 5:4*: But ye, brethren, are not in darkness, that that day should overtake "you" as a thief. *Luke 21:34:* And [take heed to yourselves], lest at any time your hearts be overcharged with surfeiting, and drunkenness, and the cares of this life, and so that day come upon "you" unawares.

Another reason why many believe in a rapture theory is because of what Jesus said to the church of Philadelphia in *Revelation 3:10*: Because thou hast kept the word of my patience, I also will keep thee from the hour of temptation, which shall come upon all the world, to try them that dwell upon the earth.

Many in the church today believe that because the Lord said this to the church of Philadelphia, this must mean that he will literally snatch his people away like a thief just before the wicked are punished for their sins. However, I believe what the Lord was referring to here was that he would keep those who have "died" [in him] from going through the hour of temptation, which would come upon the entire world, to try them that live or dwell upon the earth. The churches referred to in Revelation chapters 2 and 3 were actual churches during the time that John wrote the book of Revelation. In addition, the people who belonged to these churches at that time have since passed away to be with the Lord in spirit, sometime both during and after the life and death of John. Moreover, the Bible says that we as believers will not be resurrected and transformed until "after" God punishes the world (the wicked) for their sins. When you compare Revelation 3:10 with Isaiah 26:19-21, you will notice that God's people who have died in their faith are being told by God through the mouth of His prophet Isaiah to enter their chambers (in other words, their caskets), and to lock their doors behind them (which refers to the lids that cover their caskets), and then they are told to hide for a little moment "until" the indignation — Gods wrath upon the ungodly world — "passes." The LORD Himself shall come out of His dwelling place to punish the wicked for their sins, and the wicked shall no longer be able to hide those whom they have murdered. By bringing the dead in Christ back to life, there will be instant evidence against the wicked, as it says in *Isaiah 26:19-21:* Oh, let your dead revive! Let corpses arise! Awake and shout for joy, you who dwell in the dust! For your dew is like the dew on fresh growth; you make the land of the shades come to life. Go, my people, [enter your chambers], and [lock your doors behind you]. [Hide] but a little moment, "until" [the indignation passes]. For lo! The LORD shall come forth from His place [to punish the dwellers of the earth for their iniquity]; and [the earth shall disclose its bloodshed and shall no longer conceal its slain].

Besides that, we also have the words of the Lord Jesus himself concerning his chosen people (his elect) and how those who have died in him are not resurrected from the dead, and that we who are alive and "remain" — which should be a key word for us — are not brought back to life or changed until after the tribulation, as it says here in *Matthew 24:29-31*: Immediately "after" the tribulation of those days shall the sun be darkened, and the moon shall not give her light, and the stars shall fall from heaven, and the powers of the heavens shall be shaken: And "then" shall appear the sign of the Son of man in heaven: and "then" shall all the tribes of the earth mourn, and "they" shall see the Son of man coming in the clouds of heaven with power and great glory. And he shall send his angels with a great sound of a trumpet, and they shall gather together his "elect" from the four winds, from one end of heaven to the other.

Not only this, but also when we read scriptures like 1 Thessalonians 5:2 and 2 Peter 3:10, we somehow seem to neglect the rest of the sentence, as it says here in 2 Peter 3:10. But the day of the Lord will come as a thief in the night; [in the which] the heavens shall pass away with a great noise, and the elements shall melt with fervent heat, the earth also and the works that are therein shall be burned up.

Finally, here are two other scriptures that completely contradict the rapture theory, and they are in Mark 3 and Revelation 7. In Mark 3:27 Jesus told us that his idea of a thief is someone who first "binds" or puts down and destroys the strong man of the house and "then" spoils his goods. In addition, because we know that according to Hebrews 13:8 Jesus Christ is the same yesterday, today, and forever, we know that he wouldn't say one thing and then turn around and do another. In Revelation 7:14 we are told that those who stood before the throne of God and before the Lamb after the resurrection were those who [came out] of the great tribulation, and everyone knows that the only time you can [come out] of something, is when you are [in it]. So according to the Bible, there is no secret event called the rapture of the church.

Now concerning "The Day of the LORD," there are many references found throughout the Bible in both the Old and New Testaments that speak of this day under many different names, but they all refer to the same event. This particular day that God has set aside refers to a time when God Himself returns to earth to punish or judge the world for its sins, raise His people back to life from the dead, change those who were still alive and "remained," and then anoints His Son Jesus Christ to become King of kings and Lord of lords. Then He decrees that all nations, peoples, and tribes from every race and language under heaven that has survived His wrath by invoking His name must serve Jesus, and He will decree His Son's dominion to be an everlasting dominion and his Kingdom as one that shall not be destroyed. All throughout the Bible you will find the following words and phrases being used, but 99.5% of the time they all refer to the same event: "The Day of the LORD;" "In that day;" "and it shall come to pass in that day;" "the day of vengeance;" "the day or year of vindication for the cause of Zion or Zion's cause;" "the day of retribution;" and, "the day of His fierce anger or wrath."

3. When will the Day of the LORD take place?

The Bible says there is no one on earth who knows the exact day and hour of their return. However, it does give us a clue as to the exact year in the book of Daniel. In 1967, Israel regained control of their beloved and ancient city known as Jerusalem, after defeating their enemies all around them in a war that lasted only six days, now known as the Six Day War. Now you might ask the question, what does that have to do with the LORD'S return? Well, according to the Bible, once the nation of Israel regains control of Jerusalem, a word will go forth to begin the process of rebuilding the city, and in the book of Daniel it specifically says that the year in which they begin rebuilding the city would be exactly seventy years prior to the very day that God returns to earth with Jesus Christ in the event known as the Day of the LORD. Now, according to many rabbis that I have spoken with, the year in which they started to rebuild the city was in June of 1967. Therefore, that means the Day of the LORD will take place in 2037.

Now this may sound too good to be true, but in Daniel 9:24-27 of the Tanakh (the Jewish bible), the city will be in the rebuilding stage for sixty-two years but in a time of distress, and this distress could possibly be terrorism. During this time of terrorism there will be a gradual departure of the faith, and then at the end of the sixty-two years all these following events will occur at once: the anointed leader or Jesus Christ will "seem" to disappear and vanish or be taken out of the way (2 Thessalonians 2:7). This will cause the majority of people on earth that believed in Jesus Christ to suddenly depart from their faith in God, because it will "seem" like God is not answering their prayers spoken in his name, and that he doesn't exist. While at the same time it will seem like everyone else who lives in sin or iniquity is prospering and abounding left and right, and because of this, they will start to betray their fellow Christians, and they will start to become cold-hearted or evil-hearted like the rest of the world (Matthew 24:12 and Matthew 24:48-51). This in turn will cause an event to occur known as the great falling away or the great departure of faith that is spoken of in 2 Thessalonians 2:3. It will be a time of great testing, the purpose of which will be to try the entire world and to separate the pretenders from the chosen, where it will even be possible for those who are very close to God to abandon their faith, as it says in Luke 21:34-36 and Matthew 24:24. That is the reason why in Matthew 24:13 Jesus said that in the last days only those who endure until the very end — or in other words, only those who endure until he returns — will be saved. In Luke 18:8, Jesus gives us a clue as to the amount of unbelief there will be in the world when he returns by asking this question: "When the Son of man cometh, shall he find faith on the earth?" In addition, because the majority of people on earth will have suddenly abandoned their faith in God, they will not be concerned about the peace treaty that Israel will make at this time and how it will bring about the Day of the LORD.

When that happens, it will be the time for the man of sin, who is also referred to as the beast or the little horn in Daniel 7:11 to be revealed (2 Thessalonians 2:3). This will be the time when he will make a peace treaty with Israel for the last seven years of the seventy year period. Then after three and a half years, he will enter the temple of God erected in Jerusalem during the sixty-two year period, and he will put a stop to the daily sacrifice and meal offerings that the Jewish people have in connection with the temple. Then he will place a disgusting idol in the corner of the altar, in order to desecrate the temple of God. During this time, within the space of the last three and a half years, he will sit in the temple of God and claim to the world that he *is* God, because he will sit in the Holy of Holies where only God's presence should be. In addition, he will divide the land for profit, and he will search out and cause two-thirds of the Jewish population in Jerusalem to be murdered by fire and by sword, and to go into captivity in near-by countries. Then many families of the two-thirds will hate each other and betray each other to death. Moreover, many women during the three-and-a-half years will be raped, and if they are found to be pregnant with child, they will be dashed thru with the sword. In addition, he will also search out and persecute the one-third of the Jews who are left, of which there will be 144,000 Jewish men from every tribe of Israel who will keep themselves pure, and not defile themselves with women despite all the persecution they will endure. For keeping themselves pure while being persecuted throughout the three-and-a-half years, they will receive as their reward the name of God their Father written on their foreheads when He returns to earth, and they will be known as those who follow in the footsteps of Christ despite whatever circumstance he leads them into (Revelation 7:4 and Revelation 14:1-5).

As you can see, these last three-and-a-half years will be a time of great distress and sorrow or what the Bible refers to as the great tribulation, which mostly concerns the nation of Israel. Which will last for approximately 1,335 days from the very day that the man of sin enters the temple of God in Jerusalem and takes away the daily sacrifice and places the disgusting idol in the corner of the altar (Daniel 12:11-12). Moreover, it is during this time that the man of sin, Jerusalem, and the entire nation of Israel will be hated by all the nations of the world, because they will be seen in the eyes of all nations as troublemakers and burdensome to society. Because of all the trouble that will take place there. During the last three-and-a-half years, many Israelis will be given special revelations from God concerning the times that they will be living in, and they will then try to teach others. Many will understand them, but many will merely pretend to believe them, and many of them will be considered a threat to society for trying to teach others what they know about God and about the future, and will then be executed, and their bodies will be left lying everywhere, all around Jerusalem. However, before they are murdered, they will be taken before the representatives of the world to be judged. During the last three-and-a-half years, the armies of the nations of the world and their representatives will be surrounding the city of Jerusalem on all sides. In order to do battle with the man of sin and his army, as well as to try and take over the city of Jerusalem and to persecute Gods people (Psalms 79:1-4, Luke 21:12-24, Amos 7:17, Amos 8:2-3, Zechariah 13:8-9, Zechariah 14:2, Zechariah 12:2-3, Daniel 11:30-39, 2 Thessalonians 2:4, Mark 13:9-13, and Matthew 10:17-23). However, the nations of the world will not be able to defeat the man of sin or find him, because he will be kept safe to be burned alive by the sword of God — the river of fire that will come out of God's mouth like a flood. That he (the man of sin) will try to run away from, but eventually the fire will be poured down upon him, and upon the city, as well as upon the sculptured image that he will place in the corner of the altar. As I mentioned in part one of this chapter as well as in 2 Thessalonians 2:8, Isaiah 31:8-9, Ezekiel 43:3, Daniel 7:11, Daniel 8:25, and Revelation 13:14.

Daniel 9:24-27: "[Seventy years] have been decreed for your people and your holy city until the measure of transgression is filled and that of sin complete, until iniquity is expiated, and eternal righteousness ushered in; and prophetic vision ratified, and the Holy of Holies anointed. You must know and understand: From the issuance of the word to restore and rebuild Jerusalem *until* the [time of the] anointed leader is [seven years]; and for [sixty-two years] it will be *rebuilt,* square and moat, but in a time of [distress]. And *after* those sixty-two years, [the anointed one will disappear and vanish]. The army of [a] leader who is to come will destroy the city and the sanctuary, but [its] end will come through [a flood]. Desolation is decreed *until* the end of war. During [seven years] he will make a firm covenant with many. After three-and-a-half years, he will put a stop to the sacrifice and the meal offering. At the corner [of the altar] will be an appalling abomination until the decreed destruction will be [poured down] upon the appalling thing."

4. What will the Day of the LORD be like?

On that day, approximately 1,335 days after the man of sin enters the temple of God erected in Jerusalem during the sixty-two year period, takes away the daily sacrifice, and places the sculptured image (the Abomination of Desolation) in the corner of the altar, as I explained in answer to question three of this chapter. The first thing that will take place is a massive earthquake, one so great in magnitude that it will cover the entire earth at the same time, causing great tidal waves throughout the world, and every mountain and island on earth will literally move out of position.

The Bible says that this earthquake will take place sometime between the morning and the afternoon, Israeli time, according to Amos 8:8-9 of the Tanakh (the Jewish bible). The Bible says that God will darken the earth in the afternoon in verse 9. But in verse 8 it says He shakes [all] the earth and causes it to move back and forth and surge and subside like the Nile of Egypt because of all the evil things that will be done to the Jewish people on that day (Amos 8:1-7). Its estimated that an earthquake of this magnitude, combined with the massive tidal waves that this earthquake would create, could possibly kill almost half of the world's population if not more. The Bible also says that this earthquake will be so terrifying that the hearts of many people on earth will literally fail them because of fear, and almost everyone on earth will start to think it is the end of the world, and will start running for their lives. Running back and forth in the cities, climbing over walls, and entering into people's houses through their windows like a thief (Joel 2:9-10 and Isaiah 13:6-8). Shortly thereafter, sometime in the afternoon (Israeli time), again, according to Amos 8:9, while this earthquake is claiming the lives of millions of people on earth, there will be a sound of a great explosion in the universe that will be heard all across the world (2 Peter 3:10). Then the universe itself will literally look like its being rolled away like a scroll, because the Bible says that God Himself will make an opening in the fabric of space from His dwelling place, the New Jerusalem that is just beyond the universe, with the intense heat that comes out of His body of fire. This opening will be the cause of the great explosion that will be heard throughout the entire world. In addition, the great heat that comes out of His body of fire will continue to eat away or dissolve the rest of the elements throughout the universe, like the sun and stars and everything that gives off light and heat, and they will all be affected by it. This will cause the sun to literally shut down temporarily, the moon to not be able to reflect the light of the sun, and the stars to lose their source of power, and we are told that many stars will start falling to the earth (Isaiah 34:4, Isaiah 13:10, Joel 3:3-4, Joel 4:14-15, Matthew 24:29, Mark 13:24-25, and Revelation 6:12-14). When this happens, the nations of the world will be in great distress and perplexity, wondering what is going on. This will fulfill the words spoken of by Jesus in the gospel of Luke 21:25-26, when he said that there would be signs in the sun, in the moon, in the stars, and on the earth. As well as distress of nations with perplexity; the sea and the waves roaring; men's hearts failing them because of fear, for the powers of the universe or heaven shall be shaken.

The Bible goes on to say that everyone on earth who is still alive will be in total darkness and shall walk around like blind men (Zephaniah 1:17), because all light in the universe will be temporarily gone. At that moment, the tribes of Judah who were persecuted and caught up in the siege against Jerusalem during the great tribulation, will literally be given the ability to see in the darkness, and they will suddenly realize that God is giving them the ability to see in the dark in order to save the lives of their people. Then all around them, they will see the soldiers from every nation on earth that had come to fight against Jerusalem and to take it over, many of them on horses. Galloping around the city in great panic and madness, trying to strike at anything around them out of desperation, because they do not want the Jewish people to be able to attack them or to get away while they're in the dark. However, not realizing it, they will be attacking themselves, because of the darkness. Then during this time, the tribes of Judah will start to annihilate all the besieging peoples left and right (Zechariah 12:2-8). At that moment, when it would normally be evening in the land of Israel, there will be a sound of a great blast from the trumpet of God heard all across the earth to signal His approach. Then from the east to the west, God the Father (the Ancient of Days) will take His position as judge in the sky to punish all the nations of the world for their wickedness. With Him will be all the holy angels (also referred to as saints), which means holy beings who will descend to earth literally as flaming fire with Him and the Lord Jesus Christ from Heaven to execute judgment on the ungodly (Daniel 7:9, Isaiah 34:1-3, 2 Thessalonians 1:7-8, and Jude 14-15). Then God will light up the entire earth with the misty rays of light that stream forth from His robe of light, as well as from His lightning bolts that He will scatter throughout the world (Psalms 97:4, Psalms 104:2, Zechariah 14:6-7, and Habakkuk 3:4). In that day, the misty or hazy rays of light that comes out of His robe will surround the entire world and will cause the moon to appear to shine like the sun, and the sun to appear to shine seven times brighter than it normally does (Isaiah 30:26).

Then the kings of the earth, the elite of society, the wealthy, the leaders of the world, the powerful, every slave, and every free person who did not believe in God and did not obey the teachings of the Lord Jesus Christ. As well as everyone who bowed their knees in reverence to a sculpted image will cast their idols aside from them when they see God the Father coming down out of the sky on a blue sapphire throne covered in flames of fire and surrounded by thick dark clouds. Then as they look up and gaze at His face, one by one they will start to perish. Then all of those who did not look upon Him will notice what is happening to the people around them who did, and they will start running for their lives, and will try to hide in the caves of the mountains. Because it will be the only way for unbelievers to try and escape the fear of looking directly at His face as well as the great heat that will come out of His body of fire that will surround the entire earth and consume them while they stand on their feet, as described in Zechariah 14:12 and Psalms 21:9-10. This will also scorch the trees, and grass throughout the world and cause them to wither; the surface of every mountain and hill upon the face of the earth will melt; the rivers in the world will dry up and turn into deserts.

The lightning bolts that will come out of His hands will scatter His enemies, aiming the bolts directly at their faces. A river of sulfur and brimstone will pour out of His mouth like a flood to burn up His enemies all around Him and it will also pour down upon Jerusalem, and upon the man of sin. As well as upon the sculpted image that was placed in the corner of the altar of the temple by the man of sin during the great tribulation (Revelation 6:15-17, Exodus 33:20 and 23, Daniel 9:27, Isaiah 2:20-21, Isaiah 31:7-9, Isaiah 42:13-15, Isaiah

ANCIENT MYSTERIES OF THE BIBLE REVEALED

64:1-2, Micah 1:2-4, Psalms 97:1-7, and Psalms 21:13). The Bible says that on this day, God alone shall be exalted and He will also be glorified through Jesus Christ, who is also referred to as God's King or Majesty, as well as the Word or (Name) of God, who will represent God as King of all the earth (Isaiah 2:9-11 and Zechariah 14:9). Then as God slowly descends to earth, He will come to rest on the Mount of Olives that is near Jerusalem on the east. Then the Mount of Olives will split in two, from east to west, and one part will shift to the north and the other part will shift to the south, and it will become a huge gorge (Zechariah 14:3-4). Then the 144,000 Jewish men from every tribe of Israel, and the remainder of the one-third of the Jewish population who were persecuted and are still alive in the land of Israel, [on] the mountains and [in] the city during the great tribulation (Zechariah 13:8-9, Zechariah 14:2, Joel 3:5, Matthew 24:16, and Mark 13:14). Will see all the dead bodies of their family members who were murdered lying everywhere all over the streets of the city, who had been left there and not allowed a decent burial during the three-and-a-half years since all the nations of the world had come against Jerusalem (Psalms 79:1-7). Then the LORD will put compassion in their hearts for their family members who died, and they will all start to mourn for their dead and cry out to God concerning them, each family, or tribe by themselves, according to Zechariah 12:10-14 of the Tanakh (the Jewish bible). Moments later, the 144,000 Jewish men from every tribe of Israel will start to serve and attend to God on the Mount of Olives (Daniel 7:10).

At this time, four angels will take their places at the four corners of the earth, north, south, east, and west, preparing themselves to gather together all those who have died in Christ, after they are resurrected from the dead, as well as all those who are still alive and remain. So that they can gather them all together to greet the Lord Jesus Christ in the air, who will be entering the earth's atmosphere with Michael the archangel after all his enemies have been put down and made a footstool as promised by God his Father (Psalms 110:1, Revelation 7:1, Matthew 24:31, Mark 13:27, and 1 Thessalonians 4:16-17). However, before they begin, an angel will come from the eastern region with the seal of the living God. Which he will place on the foreheads of the 144,000 Jewish men that served and attended to Him on the Mount of Olives as their reward for keeping themselves pure and not defiling themselves with women during the great tribulation (Revelation 7:2-4 and Revelation 14:1-5). Then as soon as they are sealed, the long continuous blasting sound of the trumpet of God that was heard since the beginning of His approach to earth to announce His Presence and to strike fear and confusion in His enemies will have sounded for the "last" time (1 Corinthians 15:52). Then instantly, all those who were dead in Christ are resurrected, and all those who are alive and remained and called out to Him are changed. Then they're all caught up and gathered together in the clouds to greet the Lord in the air, wearing white robes and having palm branches in their hands. At that moment, I believe they will start to make a long procession on his right side and on his left that will stretch all the way from him to God, waving their palm branches in their hands. Similar to the way that it was for him when he entered the city of Jerusalem as described in the gospel of John 12:12-13. Because in order to be anointed as King of all the earth, he would have to be anointed King [on] the earth. At this time, his people will then present him to God and God will then anoint him to become King of kings and Lord of lords, then the glorious shout of triumph to God and Christ will sound (Revelation 7:9-10). Then God will command that all peoples from every race and language who have survived His wrath by calling out to Him must serve His Son Jesus Christ, and He will decree that His Son's dominion will be an everlasting dominion that will not pass away, and his kingship one that shall not be destroyed (Daniel 7:13-14).

As King, he will sit upon his throne, which in 1 Chronicles 29:23 is also called the throne of David, which I believe will be restored for him on this day, and he will command his angels to gather before him all the nations of the world that were left, and he will then have his angels separate the righteous from the wicked, and they will place on his left side the ungodly and his people who were just resurrected from the dead and changed on his right. Then he will explain to those on his right why they were about to enter the third Heaven (the New Jerusalem). Then he will say to those on his left, depart from me, you that are cursed or in other words headed into the path of everlasting fire that was originally prepared for Lucifer

(Satan) and his angels (Matthew 25:31-46). These people will not be cast into the lake of fire at this time, but they will be left on earth to experience the plagues that the Bible says will start falling upon the earth in Revelation 8. Then after the Lord Jesus Christ rebukes the nations, God the Father, the Lord Jesus Christ, all the holy angels, and all God's children that were resurrected and changed will depart from the earth, to enter the Kingdom of Heaven.

Here are many of the verses from the Old Testament to verify the words that I just wrote, taken from the Tanakh or the Jewish bible, to give you a better understanding of what the scriptures really mean from the Old Testament, as well as verses from the New Testament.

Amos 7:17: But this, I swear, is what the LORD said: your wives shall be ravished in the town, your sons and daughters shall fall by the sword, and your land shall be divided up with a measuring line. And you yourself shall die on unclean soil; for Israel shall be exiled from its soil.

Amos 8:1-3: This is what my Lord GOD showed me: There was a basket of summer fruit. He said, "What do you see, Amos?" "A basket of summer fruits," I replied. And the LORD said to me: "The [hour of doom] has come for My people Israel; [I will not pardon them again]. And the singing women of the palace shall howl "on that day" declares my Lord GOD: [so many corpses left lying everywhere]! Hush!"

Amos 8:8-10: Shall not the [earth] shake for this and [all] that dwell on it mourn? Shall it not [all rise] like the Nile and surge and subside like the Nile of Egypt? And "In that day" — declares my Lord GOD — I will make the sun set at [noon], I will darken the earth on a sunny day. I will turn your festivals into mourning and all your songs into dirges; I will put sackcloth on all loins and tonsures on every head. I will make the [earth] mourn as for an only child, the end of it as on a bitter day.

Isaiah 24:19-21: The earth is breaking, breaking; the earth is crumbling, crumbling. The earth is tottering, tottering; the earth is swaying like a drunkard; it is rocking to and fro like a hut. Its iniquity shall weigh it down, and it shall fall, to rise no more. "In that day" the LORD will punish the host of heaven in heaven and the kings of the earth on earth.

Isaiah 13:6-8: Howl! For the day of the LORD is near; it shall come like havoc from Shaddai. Therefore all hands shall grow limp, and all men's hearts shall sink; and, overcome by terror, they shall be seized by pangs and throes, writhe like a woman in travail. They shall gaze at each other in horror, their faces livid with fright.

2 Peter 3:10-12: But the day of the Lord will come as a thief in the night; [in the which] the heavens shall pass away with a [great noise], and the elements shall melt with fervent heat, the [earth also] and the works that are therein shall be burned up. Seeing then that all these things shall be [dissolved], what manner of persons ought ye to be in all holy conversation and godliness. Looking for and hasting unto the coming of [the day of God], wherein [the heavens being on fire shall be dissolved, and the elements shall melt with fervent heat]?

Psalms 79:1-7: O God, heathens have entered Your domain, defiled Your holy temple, and turned Jerusalem into ruins. They have left your servants' corpses as food for the fowl of heaven, and the flesh of Your faithful for the wild beasts. Their blood was shed like water [around] Jerusalem, with none to bury them. We have become the butt of our neighbors, the scorn and derision of those around us. How long, O LORD, will You be angry forever, will Your [indignation] blaze like fire? [Pour out] Your fury on the [nations] that do not know You, upon the kingdoms that do not invoke Your name, for they have devoured Jacob and [desolated] his home.

Zechariah 12:2-14: Behold, I will make Jerusalem a bowl of reeling for the peoples all around. [Judah shall be caught up in the siege upon Jerusalem, when "all the nations of the earth" gather against her]. "In that day," I will make Jerusalem a stone for all the peoples to lift; all who lift it shall injure themselves. In that day declares the LORD [I will strike every horse with panic and its rider with madness]. But [I will open the eyes of "Judah" while I strike all the peoples with blindness]. And the clans of Judah will say to themselves, "We will save the dwellers of Jerusalem with the help of their God, the LORD of Hosts." In that day, I will make the clans of Judah like a flaming brazier among sticks and like a flaming torch among sheaves. "They" shall devour all the besieging people's right and left; and Jerusalem shall continue on its site, in Jerusalem. The LORD will give victory to the tents of Judah first, so that the glory of the House of David and the glory of the inhabitants of Jerusalem may not be too great for Judah. In that day the LORD will shield the inhabitants of Jerusalem; and the feeblest of them shall be in that day like David, and the House of David like a divine being-like an angel of the LORD-at their head. In that day I will all but annihilate all the nations that came up against Jerusalem. But I will fill the House of David and the inhabitants of Jerusalem with a spirit of pity and compassion; and [they shall lament to Me about those who are slain], wailing over "them" as over a favorite son and showing bitter grief as over a first-born. In that day, the wailing in Jerusalem shall be as great as the wailing at Hadad-rimmon in the plain of Megiddo. The land shall wail, each family by itself: the family of the House of David by themselves, and their womenfolk by themselves; the family of the House of Nathan by themselves, and their womenfolk by themselves; the family of the House of Levi by themselves, and their womenfolk by themselves; the family of the Shimeites by themselves, and their womenfolk by themselves; and all the other families, every family by itself, with their womenfolk by themselves.

Zechariah 14:13-14: "In that day," a great panic from the LORD shall fall upon them, and everyone shall snatch at the hand of another, and everyone shall raise his hand against everyone else's hand. "Judah" shall join the fighting in Jerusalem, and the wealth of all the nations' roundabout-vast quantities of gold, silver, and clothing-shall be gathered in.

Isaiah 34:1-4: Approach, O nations, and listen, give heed, O peoples! Let the earth and those in it hear; the world, and what it brings forth. For the LORD is angry at [all the nations], furious at all their host; He has doomed them, consigned them to slaughter. Their slain shall be left lying, and the stench of their corpses shall mount; and the hills shall be drenched with their blood, all the host of heaven shall molder. [The heavens shall be rolled up like a scroll], and all their host shall wither like a leaf withering on the vine, or shriveled fruit on a fig tree.

Isaiah 13:9-11: Lo! The day of the LORD is coming with pitiless fury and wrath, to make the earth a desolation, [to wipe out the "sinners" upon it]. [The stars and constellations of heaven shall not give off their light]; [the sun shall be dark when it rises], and [the moon shall diffuse no glow]. And I will requite to the world its evil, and to the wicked their iniquity; I will put an end to the pride of the arrogant and humble the haughtiness of tyrants.

Isaiah 42:13-17: The LORD goes forth like a warrior, like a fighter He whips up His rage. He yells, He roars aloud, He charges upon His enemies. "I have kept silent far too long, kept still and restrained Myself; now I will scream like a woman in labor, I will pant and I will gasp. [Hills and heights will I scorch], [cause all their green to wither]; [I will turn rivers into deserts], and [dry the marshes up]. I will lead the blind by a road they did not know, and I will make them walk by paths they never knew. I will turn darkness before them to "light", [rough places into level ground]. [These are the promises-I will keep them without fail]. Driven back and utterly shamed shall be those who trust in an image, those who say to idols, "You are our gods!"

Now if you noticed where it said, I will lead the blind by a road they did not know, and I will turn darkness before them into [light]. Compare that to what it says here concerning the blind in Zephaniah 1:14-18. The great day of the LORD is approaching, approaching most swiftly. Hark, the day of the LORD! It is bitter: there a warrior shrieks! That day shall be a day of wrath, a day of trouble and distress, a day of calamity and desolation, a day of [darkness and deep gloom], a day of [densest clouds], a day of [horn blast] and alarms-against the fortified towns and the lofty corner towers. [I will bring distress on the people], and [they shall walk like blind men, because they sinned against the LORD]; their blood shall be spilled like dust, and their fat like dung. Moreover, their silver and gold shall not avail to save them. On the day of the LORD's wrath, in the fire of His passion, the whole land shall be consumed; for He will make a terrible end of all who dwell in the land.

Daniel 7:9-10, 13-14: As I looked on, thrones were set in place, and the [Ancient of Days took His seat]. His garment was like white snow, and the hair of His head was like lambs wool. His throne was tongues of flame; its wheels were blazing fire. [A river of fire streamed forth before Him]; [Thousands upon thousands served Him]; [Myriads upon myriads attended Him]; the court sat and the books were opened. As I looked on, in the night vision, one like [a human being came with the clouds of heaven]; [he reached the Ancient of Days] and [was presented to Him]. Dominion, glory, and kingship were given to him; all peoples and nations of every language must serve him. His dominion is an everlasting dominion that shall not pass away, and his kingship, one that shall not be destroyed.

If you noticed verse 10, where it says a river of fire streamed forth before Him. If you add unto this what is said in Psalms 97:3-6. Fire is His vanguard, [burning His foes on every side]. His lightning's light up the world; the earth is convulsed at the sight; mountains melt like wax at the LORD'S Presence, at the Presence of the Lord of all the earth. The heavens proclaim His righteousness and all peoples see His glory.

Micah 1:3-4: For lo! The LORD is coming forth from His dwelling-place; He will come down and stride upon the heights of the earth. [The mountains shall melt under Him and the valleys burst open-like wax before fire, like water cascading down a slope].

2 Samuel 22:7-15: In my anguish I called on the LORD, cried out to my God; in His Temple He heard my voice, my cry entered His ears. Then the earth rocked and quaked, the foundations of heaven shook-rocked by His indignation. [Smoke went up from His nostrils, from His mouth came devouring fire; live coals blazed forth from Him]. He bent the sky and came down, thick cloud beneath His feet. He mounted a cherub and flew; He was gliding on the wings of the wind. He made pavilions of darkness about Him, dripping clouds, huge thunderheads; in the brilliance before Him blazed fiery coals. The LORD thundered forth from heaven, The Most High sent forth His voice; [He let loose bolts, and scattered His enemies; lightning, and put them to rout].

Psalms 21:9-13: Your hand is equal to all your enemies; Your right hand over powers Your foes. You set them ablaze like a furnace when You show your Presence. The LORD in anger destroys them; fire consumes them. You wipe their offspring from the earth, their issue from among men. For they schemed against You; they laid plans, but could not succeed. For You make them turn back by [Your bows aimed at their face].

Zechariah 14:3-4: Then the LORD will come forth and make war on those nations as He is wont to make war on a day of battle. "On that day," He will set His feet on the Mount of Olives, near Jerusalem on the east; and the Mount of Olives shall split across from east to west, and one part of the Mount shall shift to the north and the other to the south, a huge gorge.

Isaiah 2:9-12; 19-22: But man shall be humbled, and mortal brought low-Oh, do not forgive them! Go deep into the rock, bury yourselves in the ground, before the terror of the LORD [and] His dread Majesty! Man's haughty look shall be brought low, and the pride of mortals shall be humbled. None but the LORD shall be exalted "In that day." For the LORD of Hosts has ready a day against all that is proud and arrogant, against all that is lofty-so that it is brought low. And men shall enter caverns in the rock and hollows in the ground-before the terror of the LORD [and] His dread majesty, when He comes forth to overawe the earth. "On that day," men shall fling away, to the flying foxes and the bats, the idols of silver and the idols of gold which they made for worshiping. And they shall enter the clefts in the rocks and the crevices in the cliffs, before the terror of the LORD [and] His dread majesty, when He comes forth to overawe the earth. Oh, cease to glorify man, who has only a breath in his nostrils! For by what does he merit esteem?

Joel 2:9-10: They rush up the wall, they dash about in the city; they climb into the houses, they enter like thieves by way of the windows. Before them earth trembles, heaven shakes, sun and moon are darkened, and stars withdraw their brightness.

Joel 3:3-5: [Before] the great and terrible day of the LORD comes, I will set portents in the sky and on earth: Blood and fire and pillars of smoke; the sun shall turn into darkness and the moon into blood. [But] everyone who invokes the name of the LORD shall escape; for there shall be [a remnant "On" Mount Zion and "In" Jerusalem, as the LORD promised]. [Anyone] who invokes the LORD will be among the survivors.

Joel 4:14-16: Multitudes upon multitudes in the Valley of Decision! For the day of the LORD is at hand in the Valley of

Decision. Sun and moon are darkened, and stars withdraw their brightness. And the LORD will roar from Zion, and shout aloud from Jerusalem, so that heaven and earth tremble. [But] the LORD will be a shelter to His people, a refuge to the children of Israel.

Nahum 1:2-3, 5-6: The LORD is a passionate, avenging God; The LORD is vengeful and fierce in wrath. The LORD takes vengeance on His enemies, He rages against His foes. The LORD is slow to anger and of great forbearance, [but] the LORD does not remit all punishment. He travels in whirlwind and storm, and clouds are the dust on His feet. The mountains quake because of Him, the earth heaves before Him, and the hills melt. The world and all that dwell therein. Who can stand before His wrath? Who can resist His fury? His anger pours out like fire, and rocks are shattered because of Him.

Habakkuk 3:3-7: God is coming from Teman, the Holy One from Mount Paran. His majesty covers the skies, His splendor fills the earth: It is a brilliant light which gives off rays on every side- and therein His glory is enveloped. Pestilence marches before Him, and plague comes forth at His heels. When He stands, He makes the earth shake; when He glances, He makes nations tremble. The aged-old Mountains are shattered, the primeval hills sink low. His are the ancient routes: As a scene of havoc I behold the tents of Cushan; shaken are the pavilions of the land of Midian!

John 16:22: And ye [now] therefore have [sorrow]: [but] I will see you [again], and your heart shall rejoice, and your joy no man taketh from you.

1 Thessalonians 4:17: Then we which are alive and [remain] shall be caught up together with them in the clouds, to meet the Lord in the air: and so shall we ever be with the Lord.

Matthew 24:15, 21, 29-31: When ye therefore shall see the ABOMINATION OF DESOLATION, spoken of by Daniel the prophet, stand in the holy place, (whoso readeth, let him under-stand): [For then] shall be great tribulation, such as was not since the beginning of the world to this time, no, nor ever shall be. Immediately [after] the tribulation of those days shall the sun be darkened, and the moon shall not give her light, and the stars shall fall from heaven, and the powers of the heavens shall be shaken:

[And then] shall appear the sign of the Son of man in heaven: [and then] shall all the tribes of the [earth] mourn, and they shall see the Son of man coming in the clouds of heaven with power and great glory. And he shall send his angels with a great sound of a trumpet, and they shall gather together his [elect] from the four winds, from one end of heaven to the other.

Mark 13:14, 19, 24-27: But when ye shall see the ABOMINATION OF DESOLATION, spoken of by Daniel the prophet, standing where it ought not, (let him that readeth understand), [then] let them that be in Judea flee to the mountains. For in those days shall be affliction, such as was not from the beginning of the creation which God created unto this time, neither shall be. But in those days, [after] that tribulation, the sun shall be darkened, and the moon shall not give her light, and the stars of heaven shall fall, and the powers that are in heaven shall be shaken. [And then] shall they see the Son of man coming in the clouds with great power and glory. [And then] shall he send his angels, and shall gather together his [elect] from the four winds, from the uttermost part of the earth to the uttermost part of heaven.

Luke 21:20-27: And when ye shall see Jerusalem compassed with armies, [then] know that the desolation thereof is nigh. Then let them which are in Judea flee to the mountains; and let them which are in the midst of it depart out; and let not them that are in the countries enter therein. For these be the days of vengeance, that all things which are written may be fulfilled. [But woe unto them that are with child, and to them that give suck, in those days]! For there shall be great distress in the [land], and wrath upon [this] people. And [they] shall fall by the edge of the sword, and shall be led away captive into all nations: and Jerusalem shall be trodden down of the Gentiles, until the times of the Gentiles be fulfilled. And there shall be signs in the sun, and in the moon, and in the stars; and upon the earth distress of nations, with perplexity; the sea and the waves roaring; men's hearts failing them for fear, and for looking after those things which are coming on the earth: for the powers of heaven shall be shaken. [And then] shall they see the Son of man coming in a cloud with power and great glory.

Luke 23:27-30: And there followed him a great company of people, and of women, which also bewailed and lamented him. But Jesus turning unto them said, Daughters of Jerusalem, weep not for me, but weep for yourselves, and for your children. For, behold, the days are coming, in the which they shall say, Blessed are the barren, and the wombs that never bear, and the paps which never gave suck. Then shall they begin TO SAY TO THE MOUNTAINS, FALL ON US; AND TO THE HILLS, COVER US.

1 Corinthians 15:52: In a moment, in the twinkling of an eye, at the [last] trump: for the trumpet shall sound, and the "dead" [shall be raised incorruptible], and "we" [shall be changed].

Revelation 6:12-17: And I beheld when he had opened the sixth seal, and, lo, there was a great earthquake; and the sun became black as sackcloth of hair, and the moon became as blood; and the stars of heaven fell unto the earth, even as a fig tree casteth her untimely figs, when she is shaken of a mighty wind. And the heaven departed as a scroll when it is rolled together; and every mountain and island were moved out of their places. And the kings of the earth, and the great men, and the rich men, and the chief captains, and the mighty men, and every bondman, and every free man, hid themselves in the dens and in the rocks of the mountains; and said to the mountains and rocks, Fall on us, and hide us from the [face] of Him that sitteth on the throne, [and] from the wrath of the Lamb: for the great day of his wrath is come; and who shall be able to stand?

Revelation 7:9-10, 13-17: After this I beheld, and, lo, a great multitude, which [no man] could number, of all nations, and kindred's, and people, and tongues, stood before the throne, and before the Lamb, clothed with white robes, and palms in their hands; and cried with a loud voice, saying, SALVATION TO OUR GOD WHICH SITTETH UPON THE THRONE, "AND" UNTO THE LAMB. And one of the elders answered, saying unto me, what are these which are arrayed in white robes? And whence came they? And I said unto him, sir, thou knowest. And he said to me, these are they which [came out] of great tribulation, and have washed their robes, and made them white in the blood of the Lamb. Therefore are they before the throne of God, and serve Him day and night in His temple: and He that sitteth on the throne shall dwell among them.

They shall hunger no more, neither thirst any more; neither shall the sun light on them, nor any heat. For the Lamb which is in the midst of the throne shall feed them, and shall lead them unto living fountains of waters: and God shall wipe away all tears from their eyes.

Chapter 3

The Work of the Holy Spirit

1. What is a spirit? What is the difference between spirits and the Holy Spirit? And does man really have three parts — body, soul, and spirit?

As I mentioned in chapter one, question one, every living creature in both heaven and earth that has its own mind (the ability to think), its own will (the ability to choose), and its own emotions (the ability to feel), has a spirit. A spirit is an eternal entity that can cause any inanimate object to become a living creature which then has its own mind, will, and emotions, and a spirit is itself a [part] of God. The Bible says that God is the Father of the spirits of "all" flesh (Numbers 16:22, 1 Corinthians 15:39, and Malachi 2:10).

When a Spirit first comes out of God it is Holy, which means that all Spirits, as they first come out of God are Holy Spirits, and the Holy Spirit is a child of God. However, at the same time, as they first come out of God, because they are part of His presence, they are also referred to as God, so they bear His name. In the same way children often bear the last name of their parents because they came from them. In addition, God the Father decides what His Spirits will become, what they will know and do, and what kind of body His Spirits will occupy. For example, when God began to create heaven and earth through His Word (Jesus Christ), He decided whether His Spirits would become a seraph, or a cherub, or an angel, or a human being, or an animal, or a bird, and so on. Moreover, if a Spirit remains the same and does not change by occupying a body to become a living creature, that Spirit will remain a Holy Spirit. But once a Spirit occupies a body, that spirit is no longer called the Holy Spirit, but will become whatever that creature is, whether it remains in that creature's body or not. That is the reason why all living creatures, whether they are seraphs, cherubs, angels, human beings, animals, birds, fish, and so forth, though they all have spirits, their spirits are not referred to as the Holy Spirit. They are referred to as the spirits of human beings, the spirits of beasts, the spirits of fallen angels or demons, and so on.

There are many theologians who teach that man has three parts, body, soul, and spirit, and it is the soul of man, not his spirit that has his mind, will, and emotions. But according to the Bible, that would imply that man's soul is capable of being manipulated or destroyed, because everyone knows that during times of war man has been known to have the ability to manipulate and destroy the mind and will of others, by causing someone and forcing someone to do things that they didn't want to do. But according to Matthew 10:28, Jesus said that a man's soul cannot be touched, harmed or destroyed by another man. So whenever there is a reference to a man's soul, his breath of life, or his ghost, it always refers to that part of man that causes him to be a living being, with the "ability" to think, choose, and feel — what is also referred to as his spirit. For example, the Bible says the Holy Ghost is called the Holy Spirit or the Spirit of God. In addition, the Spirit of God is called the breath of life or the breath of God. Moreover, in Genesis 2:7, when God placed the breath of life or His Spirit into man, He did not put another entity in man besides His Spirit that is referred to as the soul. Therefore, the breath of life or the spirit in man is also called the soul in man. Here are a few examples in the Bible that speak of man's soul, his breath of life, his spirit, and his ghost as being the same thing, and where it is the "spirit" in man, not another entity in him called the soul that has his mind, will, and emotions.

In *Job 32:8* it says, but truly it is the [spirit] in men, [the breath of Shaddai], that gives them understanding. In Matthew 26:41 we read, watch and pray that ye enter not into temptation: the [spirit] indeed is willing, but the flesh is weak. In *Revelation 6:9-11* it says, "and when he had opened the fifth seal, I saw under the altar the [souls of them] that were slain for the word of God, and for the testimony which they held: and they cried with a loud voice, saying, How long, O Lord, holy and true, dost thou not judge and avenge our blood on them that dwell on the earth? And [white robes] were given unto every one of them; and it was said unto them, that they should rest yet for a little season, until their fellow servants also and their brethren, that should be killed as they were, should be fulfilled."

Now, if it was true that a person's soul was just his mind, will, and emotions, then how could that soul wear a white robe? Furthermore, if you consider also that Jesus himself said that a man's spirit and his soul are one and the same. In that a spirit or any spirit has the ability to think, choose, and feel, as it says here concerning an evil spirit or demon in Matthew 12:43-45: "When the unclean spirit is gone out of a man, he walketh through dry places, seeking rest, and findeth none. Then he saith, I will return into my house from whence I came out; and when he is come, he findeth it empty, swept, and garnished. Then goeth he, and taketh with himself seven other spirits more wicked than himself, and they enter in and dwell there: and the last state of that man is worse than the first. Even so shall it be also unto this wicked generation."

The first thing you may have noticed is the mind of that evil spirit, when he thinks to himself that he should go back to the body that he came out from, even claiming ownership to that person's body by saying "my house" (which ownership was only possible because that person was living in sin). The second thing you can see is that spirit's will in action when he chooses seven other spirits more wicked than himself to be his room mates. In addition, the third thing that you may have noticed is the emotions of that spirit, when Jesus said the spirit had the emotion of evil or wickedness.

2. What does the Holy Spirit look like? And what is his assignment from God?

Many theologians have tried to describe the Holy Spirit's physical appearance in many different ways. Some say he is fire, others say he is wind, while others say he has the shape of a human being. Though all that is true, many do not know or understand the process or the stages of development that a Holy Spirit goes through when he first comes out of God the Father.

In the Bible, whenever a Holy Spirit first comes out of God, he physically resembles a piece of fire, sort of like that little piece of fire that you see jumping out of a campfire at night. But in this case, the Holy Spirit is literally a piece of fire that comes out of God Himself, who is a being of fire, which makes him literally a [part] of God, as I mentioned in chapter one in answer to question one. So if you could imagine a piece of fire coming out of God, who is a being of fire, this is what the Holy Spirit looks like. However, to get an even more accurate description of what he looks like in detail, a good place to start is in Revelation. In Revelation 4:5 John describes seeing seven of these pieces of fire hovering in mid-air before the throne of God, which the Bible refers to as the Holy Spirits, as seven lamps of fire. But to understand what John meant when he described them as seven (lamps of fire), we must turn to Ezekiel chapter 1, where Ezekiel describes seeing these same Spirits hovering before God's throne as being burning coals of fire resembling torches or flares, which explains why John referred to them as (lamps of fire). It is important to remember that in John's time, as well as in Ezekiel's time, torches were often used as lamps, as it says here in Ezekiel 1:13-14. Such then was the appearance of the creatures. With them was something that looked like [burning coals of fire]. This fire, suggestive of [torches], kept moving about [among] the creatures; the fire had radiance, and lightning issued from the fire. Dashing to and fro [among] the creatures was something that looked like flares. For this very reason, because they are called burning coals of fire, they are also referred to as the stones of fire in Ezekiel 28:14.

So according to Ezekiel, this is most likely what John saw in his vision when he described them as seven (lamps of fire). However, the Bible goes on to say that when John was granted a closer look at them in Revelation 5:6, he describes the Lamb of God or Jesus Christ standing in front of God's throne with them. In addition, he said that each one of them had an eye in the center of its coal, and the long flame of fire upon each one of them that resembled a torch or flare from a distance had the shape of a horn, as it says here in Revelation 5:6. And I beheld, and, lo, in the midst of the throne and of the four beasts, and in the midst of the elders, stood a Lamb as it had been slain, having [seven horns and seven eyes], "which are" [the seven Spirits of God] sent forth into all the earth.

The Bible also says that when a Holy Spirit first comes out of God, he has the ability to literally transform himself into wind or any shape and then back again into fire. As it says here when they made their first appearance after Christ's resurrection in *Acts 2:2-3:* "And suddenly there came a sound from heaven as of a rushing mighty [wind], and *it* [filled all the house where they were sitting]. And there appeared unto them [cloven tongues like as of fire], and *it* [sat upon] each of them." *Job 4:15-17:* "A [wind] passed by me, making the hair of my flesh bristle. *It* halted; [its appearance was strange to me]; a [form] loomed before my eyes; I heard a murmur, a voice, can mortals be acquitted by God? Can man be cleared by his Maker?

In the second stage of a Holy Spirit's development, whenever it first enters a body to become a living creature, whether it's the body of a human being, an animal, and so on, in order to make it a living creature that spirit will then take on the shape of that creature's body to represent the body it's in. An example of this is in Revelation 6:9-11, where the Bible speaks of the souls or spirits of those killed for the word of God and for their good testimony. And how [white robes] were given to each one of them, because their spirits or souls had the shape or form of the bodies that they occupied on earth.

The Bible says that the Holy Spirit has two assignments from God. The first assignment concerns the seven main Spirits that hover before His throne. Each one of them has the assignment of going into all the earth, according to Revelation 5:6 and imparting [any gift], the Father sends them to impart, as it says here in *1 Corinthians 12:7-11:* "But the manifestation of the Spirit is given to every man to profit withal. For to one is given by the Spirit the word of wisdom; to another the word of knowledge by the "same" Spirit; to another faith by the "same" Spirit; to another the gifts of healing by the "same" Spirit; to another the working of miracles; to another prophecy; to another discerning of Spirits; to another divers kinds of tongues; to another the interpretation of tongues: but all these worketh that [one and the "selfsame" Spirit], dividing to every man severally as he will."

The second assignment of the Holy Spirit concerns you and me. Whenever a person becomes a born again believer in Jesus Christ, a new Holy Spirit comes out of God the Father, enters that person's body, and becomes one with that person's spirit. It will remain in that person forever, as long as that person remains one with God or in right standing with Him, as it says here in *John 15:26*: "But when the Comforter is come, whom I will send unto you from the Father, even the Spirit of truth, which [proceedeth from the Father], he shall testify of me." *1 Corinthians 6:17*: "But he that is joined unto the Lord is [one spirit]." *John 17:21*: "That *they* all may be [one]; as thou, Father, [art *in* me], and [I *in* thee], that *they* also may be [one *in* us]: that the world may believe that thou hast sent me.

On the other hand, if that person does not remain one with God or in right standing with Him, the new Holy Spirit that is sharing residency with that person's own human spirit will be taken away from him on the day of the LORD's return, according to Ephesians 4:30, and will still remain a Holy Spirit.

3. What part does the Holy Spirit have in God's plan of salvation?

This may be a surprise to many, but the Holy Spirit, not Jesus Christ, is actually the foundation for God's entire plan of salvation. Because if God the Father could not create or give birth to other Spirits, there would be no animals, no human beings, no Jesus Christ, no angels, no cherubs, no fallen angels, and no Satan — only God Himself. Even Jesus said in John 8:42 that he was a Spirit who literally came out from God like all other Spirits. Jesus said unto them, "if God were your Father, ye would love me: for [I proceeded forth] and came from God; [neither came I of myself], but *He* sent me."

It is interesting to note that when the Jews accused Jesus of blasphemy in John 10:31-36, just because he said that he was the Son of God. Jesus reminded them of the scripture in Psalms 82:1-7, where it says that God addresses all of His spirits (His children) who do what is right in His eyes as having the right to be called divine beings or little gods — in other words, children or gods of the "Most High God" or God the Father. This is sort of like saying that animals give birth to other animals, human beings give birth to other human beings, and God gives birth to other gods. That is the reason why, as I mentioned in chapter one question one, you will never find Jesus plainly saying that he is the Father or that he is God. But you will find Jesus saying that the [only] true God is God the Father Himself, and that *he* (Jesus Christ), is the one that God sent into the world to redeem humanity back to Himself. Moreover, here is an example where the Holy Spirit, who is a son, a child, an offspring of God, can be seen as the foundation for God's entire plan of salvation.

In John 17:1-11, you will see the Holy Spirit speaking to God the Father *through* Jesus Christ and saying to Him Father, the time has come (the hour has come); glorify Your Son. In other words, glorify one of Your Spirits, the one that is occupying the person of Jesus Christ, and the one that You have given power over all flesh to, *so that* he may give eternal life to as many as You have given him. And this is life eternal, that they might know *You* (God the Father), as the *only* true God, and Jesus Christ, the one whom *You* sent. Then in verse six he says to the Father, "I have revealed Your name to the men who You gave to me out of the world: they were Yours, and You gave them to me; and they have kept Your word." Then in verse eight he says to the Father, "I have given them the words that You gave to me, and they have received them, and have known for sure that [I came out from You], and they believe that You did send me." Then in verse eleven, he tells the Father to keep them in His own name, that they may be one with him and the Father again, as it says here:

John 17:1-11: "These words spake Jesus, and lifted up his eyes to heaven, and said, Father, the hour has come; glorify thy Son, that

ANCIENT MYSTERIES OF THE BIBLE REVEALED

thy Son also may glorify thee: as [thou hast given him power over all flash], "that" he should give eternal life to as many as thou hast given him. And this is life eternal, that they might know "thee" [the only true God], and Jesus Christ, whom thou hast sent. I have glorified thee on the earth: I have finished the work which thou gavest me to do. And now, O Father, glorify thou me with thine own self with the glory which I had with thee before the world was. I have manifested thy name unto the men which thou gavest me out of the world: [thine they were], and [thou gavest them me]; and they have kept thy word. Now they have known that all things whatsoever thou hast given me are of thee. For I have given unto them the words which thou gavest me; and they have received them, and have known surely that [I came out from thee], and they have believed that thou didst send me. I pray for them: I pray not for the world, but for them which thou hast given me; for they are thine. And all mine are thine, and thine are mine; and I am glorified in them. And now I am no more in the world, but these are in the world, and I come to thee. Holy Father, keep through thine own name those whom [thou hast given me, that they may be one, as we are]."

Chapter 4

The Lamb of God: Our Elder Brother

∽◦∾

1. If there is only *one* God, who is Jesus Christ? And what makes him different from Mohammed, Buddha, and Confucius?

As I mentioned in chapter one, questions one and two, God is a massive and visible Spirit being of everlasting fire, and any creature that goes too close to Him that is not clean physically and spiritually, whether man or beast, would not be able to survive in His presence.

For this reason, ever since man first sinned against God in the Garden of Eden, God knew that humanity would never be able to survive and co-exist with Him at the same time, because He knew that it was not possible for man to separate himself from his sinful nature once his nature became corrupted by sin. Furthermore, because He is a righteous and just God, He will not allow evil and chaos to continue forever. Therefore, when God first revealed Himself to Moses and the ancient Israelites on Mount Sinai, His first attempt was to reveal to them His plan of salvation by means of a blood covenant, by commanding them to sacrifice kosher or clean animals to Him as a means of atonement for their sins. However, God knew that this would only be temporary, in terms of salvation, because He knew that it was not possible for the blood of bulls and goats to satisfy His requirement for the salvation of humankind. Moreover, because there was no one on earth who was pure who could die in man's place – due to the sinful nature that was passed down from Adam — God decided to reveal His blood covenant more clearly. By sacrificing Himself like a sacrificial Lamb *through* His Holy Spirit in the person of Jesus Christ, who was placed into the body of Christ by God without measure and with an unlimited amount of knowledge concerning the things of God since his birth, in order to redeem humanity back to Himself. *John 1:29*: "The next day John seeth Jesus coming unto him, and saith, Behold the Lamb of God, which taketh away the sin of the world." *John 3:34*: For *he* whom God hath sent [speaketh the words of God]: for God giveth not the Spirit by measure unto *him*. 2 *Corinthians 5:19*: "To wit, that God was *in* Christ, reconciling the world unto *Himself,* not imputing their trespasses unto them; and hath committed unto us the word of reconciliation. *Hebrews 9:14*: How much more shall the blood of Christ, who *through* [the eternal Spirit] offered himself without spot [to God], purge your conscience from dead works to serve the living God?"

The prophet Isaiah in Isaiah 7:14 prophesied it many years ago before the birth of Christ, that the sign of God's arrival to redeem humanity back to Himself "through" His Holy Spirit in the person of Jesus Christ would be through a virgin birth. As it also says here in *Matthew 1:22-23*: Now all this was done, that it might be fulfilled which was spoken of the Lord by the prophet, saying, BEHOLD, A *VIRGIN* SHALL BE WITH CHILD, AND SHALL BRING FORTH A SON, AND THEY SHALL CALL HIS NAME EMMMANUEL, which being interpreted is, God with us."

Besides being God's plan of salvation, there are **seven** key things that separate Jesus Christ from Mohammed, Buddha, Confucius, and every other religious figure in world history. **First,** he is called the only "begotten" Son of God, because he is the only one who did not have a natural father. So that made God his natural Father, as well as the Father of his spirit, as it says here in *John 1:14*: And the word was made flesh, and dwelt among us, (and we beheld his glory, the glory as of the [only] "begotten" of the Father), full of grace and truth."

Second, whenever the Bible says that Jesus Christ is the Son of God, you will always find the word "Son" spelled with a capital S for him. Because according to John 17:2, God the Father placed him

(Jesus Christ) in a higher position than "all" flesh. In other words, higher in position and authority than all of His other sons or spirits, whether they are angels, cherubs, human beings, and so on, so that anyone who God "through" His Holy Spirit leads to him (Jesus Christ), will be given eternal life.

Third, because God is using him and *only* him to redeem humanity back to Himself, he is also called the mediator and the anointed one in Luke 4:14-21, that has been anointed by God to be the [go between] of God and man, to represent both sides. For this reason he is often referred to as the "Son" of man to represent man, and he is often referred to as the Lord "God" to represent God the Father, as it says here in *1 Timothy 2:5*: For there is *one* God, and *one* [mediator] *between* God and men, the *man* Christ Jesus.

Fourth, he also allowed himself to be worshiped in John 20:28, because he is God's future King who will rule over God's people on behalf of God forever, which is why he also referred to himself as our Master and Lord in John 13:13. There was a time when the nation of Israel had only God as their King (1 Samuel 12:12), but because they were rebellious and had no earthly king after the flesh to reign over them and to set things in order like the other nations of the world, everyone just did as they pleased (see Judges 17:6). However, when God understood the desire of His people, and how much they wanted an earthly king to reign over them like the other nations of the world. He warned them of all the things that a king would make them do, and that what they were asking for was something very wicked in His sight, because they wanted a human king instead of Him (1 Samuel 8:4-9; 12:17). Nevertheless, God did grant them their wish, and ever since then there have been many kings who've reigned over Israel on God's behalf. However, God made a promise to the nation of Israel through His prophets that someday He would give them a King after His own heart like unto King David. A King who would rule over them as the future King of Israel forever, a King who would represent Him, a King who would be "named" God's plan of grace and God the Father's peaceable ruler as it says in *Isaiah 9:5-6*: "For a *child* has been born to us, a *son* has been given us. And *authority* has settled on *his* shoulders. He has been *named* – 'The mighty God is planning grace; the Eternal

Father, a peaceable ruler' — in token of abundant authority and of peace without limit upon David's throne and kingdom, *that* [it may be firmly established in justice and in equity] now and evermore. The zeal of the LORD of Hosts shall bring this to pass."

Micah 5:1-3: And you, O Bethlehem of Ephrath, least among the clans of Judah, from you [one] shall come forth to rule Israel [for Me]-One whose *origin* is from of old [from ancient times]. Truly, God will leave them [helpless] *until* [she] who is to bear has borne; then the rest of *his* countrymen shall return to the children of Israel. *He* shall stand and shepherd by the *might* of the LORD, by the power of the *name* of the LORD *his* God, and they shall dwell [secure]. For lo, *he* shall wax great to the ends of the earth.

Fifth, he is the prophet that Moses spoke of in Deuteronomy 18:15-19. Who was also reaffirmed by Peter to be that prophet mentioned in Acts 3:22-23: "For Moses truly said unto the fathers, a prophet shall the LORD your God raise up unto you of your brethren, like unto me; "him" shall ye hear in [all things] whatsoever he shall say unto you. And it shall come to pass that every soul, which will not hear that prophet, shall be destroyed from among the people."

Sixth, he is also called the Alpha and Omega, the first, and the last, in Isaiah 48:12 and Revelation 1:8 and 11. As I mentioned in chapter one, the Bible says that before the world was created, he was the "first" Holy Spirit to be born of God or to come out of God. Just like all other Holy Spirits after him that came out of God during the creation of the world to become living creatures (see Colossians 1:15, John 17:5 and 8, John 8:42, and John 16:27). He was also the same Spirit that hovered over what I believe to have been the water of life that proceeds from the throne of God (Genesis 1:2). With whom God created heaven, earth, and all things (Genesis 1:2-26). When God said to him, "Let there be light," "Let there be an expanse," "Let the dry land appear," and so forth. This also explains why he is called the Word of God in Hebrews 11:3, Isaiah 48:12-16, and Colossians 1:15-17. He is also referred to as the "last" because he became the first man to have ended the power of death by being the first to be resurrected from the dead (Colossians 1:18 and 1 Corinthians 15:20). So that again, God could place him (Jesus Christ), His first born Son, in a position higher than all flesh and all things created, and to have power over them, in order to fill all things as described in Colossians 1:19, Matthew 28:18, and John 17:2. Notice what he says in Revelation concerning how he is the last by being the first to rise from the dead:

Revelation 1:17-18: "And when I saw him, I fell at his feet as dead. And he laid his right hand upon me, saying unto me, fear not; I am the first and the [last]. I am he that *liveth*, and *was* dead; and, behold, [I am alive for evermore], Amen; and [have the keys of hell and of death]."

Moreover, the **seventh** characteristic that separates Jesus Christ from every other religious figure in history is that Jesus is our Elder Brother. In the gospel of Luke 15:11-32, Jesus tells the story of a man who had two sons, one who would always do his father's will, and the other who was tired of doing his father's will and ran off to do his own and to spend his entire fortune on lustful pleasures. But when he reached a certain point in his life when he had lost everything, he remembered that he still had his father and his family, and this gave him hope. So he went back to his father's house to beg for his forgiveness, so at least he could still be a part of his father's family. However, when he went back to his father's house, his father received him with open arms and made a celebration for him, because His son who had been lost was now found. But the Bible goes on to say that the elder brother became angry, because he spent all of his life doing his father's will and he never once sinned against his father, and yet not once was a celebration made in his honor, but yet his father made a celebration for his younger brother who **had** sinned against their father. He felt that this was not fair, so he would not rejoice over his brother. Therefore, the Father came out of the celebration and said to his oldest Son, "you are always with me, and all that I have is yours. But it was only right that we should celebrate over your brother, because he was lost, and now he is found."

Some believe this story is like a metaphor of the Gentiles who come to Jesus as being the youngest son who was lost and found, and the Jewish people as the older brother. There are those who think the attitude of the elder brother was very sinful, so it matches the unbelief that many Jewish people have had toward God throughout

ANCIENT MYSTERIES OF THE BIBLE REVEALED

history as well as the attitude they have had toward the Gentiles coming into the family of God through Jesus Christ.

But if you read it very carefully, you will find that the older brother in this story did not sin just because he was angry, because the Bible says that anger alone is not sin, and that there is such a thing as righteous anger, where in righteousness you hate the evil things that others do (Ephesians 4:26; Proverbs 8:13). Besides this, many have overlooked a few things in this story. Throughout this story you will notice that the father's two sons, the oldest and the youngest, are both spelled with a lower case s, but in verse 31 the Father's oldest Son is spelled with a capital S. Moreover, as I mentioned earlier, the only time you will see the word "Son" spelled with a capital S is when it refers to Jesus Christ. In addition, in verse 29, the oldest Son says to his Father that he has never transgressed or broken any of his Father's commandments, and in verse 31, the Father tells His oldest Son that he is always with Him, and all that He has is his. Therefore, in this story, Jesus was telling us all along that he was, and is, our Elder Brother. This also explains why he referred to us as his "brethren" in John 20:17. Through this story, we also have an understanding of how he may have felt about us at times and that there must have been times that he felt that we didn't deserve to have him die on the cross and redeem us back to the Father through his death. Which in fact we did not; we deserved death and nothing less. But thanks be to God that Jesus Christ our Elder Brother loved us so much that he decided to sacrifice his life and do the Father's will and not his own, and to pay the price for our sins, for which we as believers are eternally grateful.

2. What is the biblical millennium? And what will this millennium be like before, during, and at the end?

The biblical millennium refers to a thousand years of universal happiness. The Bible says that in the future, Jesus Christ will reign on this earth in a natural Jerusalem for a thousand years as King of kings and Lord of lords. In Revelation 20:4-5 and 21:1, we read how this will take place before God creates the new heaven and the new earth.

Jesus often referred to this millennium as the time of "regeneration." The Bible says there will be two kinds of people living on the earth during this time: the children of the resurrection, those who can never die again (Luke 20:36). As well as those who were still alive and not resurrected at his return, but who were changed (transformed) during the resurrection. As it says in *1 Corinthians 15:52*: "In a moment, in the twinkling of an eye, at the last trump: for the trumpet shall sound, and the *dead* [shall be raised incorruptible], and *we* [shall be changed]." These people who are still alive when Christ appears will still be mortal and thus will die a natural death. However, instead of only being able to live past a hundred, their bodies will be able to literally regenerate for a thousand years, as it says here in *Isaiah 65:20-22*: "No more shall there be an infant or graybeard that does not live out his days. [He who dies at a hundred years shall be reckoned a youth], and [he who fails to reach a hundred shall be reckoned accursed]. They shall build houses and dwell in them; they shall plant vineyards and enjoy their fruit. They shall not build for others to dwell in, or plant for others to enjoy. [For the days of My people shall be as long as the days of a tree], My chosen ones shall wear out the work of their hands."

The Bible says that just before the start of the millennium, the universe (the second heaven) will split open and Jesus Christ and his armies will be seen coming down out of the sky on white horses to wage war against the Antichrist and his false prophet. As well as the leaders of the world and all the nations that they represent, who had accepted the mark of the Beast. Then the armies of the Lord that followed him on white horses will annihilate the majority of the people on earth. But the rest of the world will be consumed by the sword of fire that will pour out of the Lord's mouth, much like the river of fire that will pour out of God's mouth when He returns to earth in the event known as the Day of the LORD. In addition, the corpses of all the nations of the world will be left as a sacrificial feast for the vultures of the sky to consume, which is described in Revelation 19:11-21. After this, Satan will then be cast into the bottomless pit of darkness (also referred to as hell), so that he will not be able to deceive the nations of the world into making war with each other again until the thousand years are completed (Revelation 20:1-3). After Satan's imprisonment, the nations of the world that fought against Jerusalem during the great tribulation. And survived when the LORD returned to earth in the Day of the LORD, will make a pilgrimage to Israel to help the Israelites rebuild the natural Jerusalem and the temple that is to be built for the Lord Jesus Christ for his millennial reign. Then Jesus Christ, who is also referred to as the Branch, will direct the entire building process. Then when it is completed, he will sit on his throne and rule from Jerusalem for a thousand years. During his reign, the nations of the world will make a pilgrimage to Jerusalem once a year to worship the Lord and to keep the feast of tabernacles. Moreover, any nation that does not go up to Jerusalem once a year to appear before the Lord will be punished and will be given no rain for their crops and other livelihood, except for the Egyptians, who will be punished in a different manner as described in Isaiah 60:10, Zechariah 6:15, and Zechariah 14:16-19.

During Christ's reign, God will then make it up to every believer who gave up everything they had to follow Jesus, by giving them a hundred-fold return on everything they might have lost and a thousand years to enjoy it. Then when the thousand years are over, He will create the new heaven and the new earth, in which they will all be given everlasting life (Matthew 19:28-29). As well as what it says in *Luke 18:29-30*: "And he said unto them, verily I say unto you, there is no man that hath left house, or parents, or brethren, or wife, or children, for the kingdom of God's sake, who shall not receive manifold more [in this present time] and [in the world to come life everlasting]."

At the close of the millennium, Satan will be released out of his prison of darkness to deceive the nations of Gog in the northern part of the world, those who dwell in the land of Magog. By putting evil thoughts of envy and hatred in their minds concerning those that are blessed in the land of Israel. At that moment, the nation of Gog will then try to make for themselves weapons of war in order to annihilate the Israelites. However, because the millennium had been a time of peace, there will not be any way for them to develop major weapons like guns, missiles, and such. Therefore, the only weapons that will be available to them will be things like clubs, spears, shields, bows, and arrows. Nevertheless, as they approach the mountains of Israel, God the Father will rise up in anger and rain down sulfurous fire out of the sky, in much the same way that it will be done on the Day of the LORD. He will strike the bows out of their left hand and will loosen the arrows from their right. At that point, their flesh and blood will then become a sacrificial feast for the carrion birds and the wild beasts of the field. In addition, while the animals and birds are eating their corpses, God will rain down fire upon those who stood behind in the land of Magog, because they were part of the conspiracy to annihilate Israel. After this, the LORD will then look upon Satan, and Satan will realize that his time is over, and the LORD will then have him cast into the lake of fire where the beast and the false prophet are, and they will be tormented day and night forever and ever (Revelation 20:7-10). Then after the animals and birds are done eating and drinking their fill of flesh and blood, the inhabitants of Israel will go out and make fires with the weapons that they find on the ground, and they will use them as fuel for their fires for seven years. They will be commanded not to cut down any tree in the forest, because God will want them to use the weapons on the ground as fuel for their fires in order to get rid of them. The Israelites will spend seven months burying the bones of Gog in order to cleanse the land. Moreover, all the bones will be gathered and buried in one place, and the name of that place will be the City of Multitude as described in Ezekiel 38:1-23 and 39:1-16.

3. What is the resurrection of the dead? What kind of body will a person receive at the resurrection? And how many resurrections will there be?

The word resurrection literally means to restore to life, to reanimate, renew, reconstruct, and to bring back from the dead. The Bible says that even if we are dead, one day God Himself through His Spirit will resurrect all those who were dead in Christ and restore them back to life, in the same way that He resurrected Christ himself from the dead. The Bible says that He has also given this power to our Lord Jesus Christ, as it says here in *John 11:25*: "Jesus said unto her, I am the resurrection, and the life: he that believeth in me, though he *were* dead, yet shall he live."

To understand what happens to a person during the resurrection of the dead, and to understand what kind of body a person will receive, we must first understand something about God. In Ecclesiastes 3:14 the Bible says that whatever God does, He does it to last forever. So when God reanimates the dead back to life, He literally puts the bodies back together again, and the bodies' cellular structure of flesh and bone will then become permanent or immortal. However, many theologians say that the body a person receives at the resurrection will be a spiritual body, and though this is true, it will not be a spirit type of body but simply an eternal one— in other words, a spiritual transformation of the natural body. In Luke 24:39, when the disciples saw Jesus after his resurrection, they saw him with the same body of flesh and bone that bore the scars of his crucifixion. This tells us that the resurrected body will not be transparent, and it will not be a completely different type of flesh, but it will be the same flesh-and-bone body, yet different in that it will be reconstructed by God Himself through His Spirit, which will make it an eternal, flesh-and-bone body.

Because if this is not the case, we must ask ourselves two questions: if the resurrected body will be a completely different type of flesh, what did God do with the body that bore the scars of Jesus' crucifixion? And how did Jesus get the same scars on his new body that had been placed on his crucified body?

I believe the answer to these questions can be found in 1 Corinthians 15:44, where the apostle Paul gave us a clue as to what kind of body the resurrected body will be by giving us two words: "sown" and "raised." From those two words, we conclude that the body will be "sown" or put into the ground or grave as a natural body; and "it" meaning the same body, will be "raised" as an eternal or spiritual body. As it says here in 1 Corinthians 15:44: *It* is *sown* a natural body; *it* is *raised* a spiritual body. There is a natural body, and there is a spiritual body. However, unlike the scars that Jesus has on his body from his crucifixion, our bodies will be made completely whole and without any blood, because blood is corruptible, as described in 1 Corinthians 15:50. This tells us that the resurrected body of Christ did not have any blood as well. In addition, because the resurrected body's cellular structure will never age or die, a person's body of flesh and bone will be able to hold massive amounts of energy and light, as compared to someone who has a body that is still capable of dying from just the slightest amount of radiation. This will make it possible for the resurrected body to do amazing things, like transcend time and space. This explains why Jesus was able to pass through walls and be in one place and then appear in another, because of the massive amount of concentrated energy and light that came from the Holy Spirit inside of his resurrected body (John 20:26; Luke 24:30-31).

The Bible says there will be two resurrections. The first resurrection takes place at three different times. The first time it takes place is during the day of the LORD's return. In the first part of the first resurrection, all those who are still alive when Christ appears will not be resurrected, but they will be changed (transformed) in such a way as to be able to live and reign with Christ for a thousand years during the millennium. Before they are given eternal life in the new heaven and earth to come, as I mention in part two of this chapter. However, all those who were dead in Christ will be brought back to life and will never be able to die again, as I mentioned earlier, for they will become immortal like the angels. As it says here in *Luke 20:36*: "Neither can they die anymore: for [they are equal unto the angels]; and are the children of God, being [the children of the resurrection]."

However, there is also a horrifying story to the first part of the first resurrection as well. The Bible says that on this day, any individual who had given their life to Jesus Christ while they lived, but did not repent of their sins before they died, this individual will be resurrected back to life the same way as everyone else. But, after he receives his immortal body of flesh and bone, he will then be found naked, not wearing a wedding garment, which is actually a white linen robe that says a person is righteous (Revelation 19:8). When the Lord sees this person naked, he will command his angels to bind him and cast him into outer darkness (commonly referred to as hell). Where he will be in such emotional pain and physical agony, because of the heat that comes from the thick dark smoke that fills its caverns, that he will grind his teeth from the torment (Matthew 22:1-13, Daniel 12:2, and John 5:28-29).

In the second part of the first resurrection, all those who were beheaded during the reign of the Antichrist will be resurrected back to life and judged, just before the start of the millennium, and they will reign with Christ for a thousand years (Revelation 20:4). In the third part of the first resurrection, all those who have died during the millennium, which refers to those who were still alive and not resurrected at the return of Christ, but who were changed (transformed) in order for them to live and reign with Christ for a thousand years during the millennium, as described in Isaiah 65:20-23. Will not be able to live again until the thousand years are finished, as it says here in *Revelation 20:5*: "[But the rest of the dead] *lived* not again *until* [the thousand years were finished]. *This is* [the first resurrection]."

The Bible also says that in the third part of the first resurrection, all those who died in Christ during the millennium and did not live again until "after" the millennium will be judged at the great white throne of judgment, as described in Revelation 20:12, just before those coming out of hell in Revelation 20:13. This is where the first resurrection will be immediately divided from the second. Because if you read Revelation 20:11-15, you will notice that *before* hell delivers up the dead that was in it to be judged in verse 13, there were already people who had just been brought back to life from the dead and were being judged in verse 12. Moreover, if you consider that in the Bible, only those who have died and gone to "hell" will face a second death. Then those people who were being judged in verse 12, are part of the first resurrection. Not only this, but when the Bible says that "whosoever" was not found written in the book of life was cast into the lake of fire, this is implying that at the great white throne of judgment there were people who *were* found written in the book of life in verse 12, by saying "whosoever" was not found. Therefore, the second resurrection — that holds the power of the second death — will start during the great white throne of judgment in Revelation 20:13. Where all those who have died in their sins and gone to "hell," whether they died in the ocean or on land, will be brought back to life with a renewed flesh-and-bone body and will then be cast *alive* into the lake of fire.

Chapter 5

Israel: The Children of God

ᏰᎧᏰ

1. Who was Abraham? And what was the covenant that God made with him and his descendents?

Besides the name of Jesus Christ, there is no other name throughout history that has been associated with what it means to have faith in God as the name of Abraham. But who was Abraham? And what was his real ethnicity? There are many who say that Abraham was the father of the Hebrews. Though that is true, it was not his real ethnicity.

The Bible says that Abram, who we now refer to as "Abraham" because of the everlasting covenant that God made with him, was a Chaldean by birth. When Abram's father Terah was seventy years old, he took his son Abram, his grandson Lot, and his daughter-in-law Sarai out of their native land of Ur, which was home to the Chaldeans, and set out for the land of Canaan. However, before they reached Canaan, Abram's father Terah passed away in the land of Haran at the age of 205 (see Genesis 11:26-32). After the passing of Abram's father, the LORD told Abram to continue his journey on from his native land and from the house of his father Terah, to the land that God would assign for him, which would come to be known as the land of Canaan; because it would be there that the LORD would make of him a great nation (see Genesis 12:1-2). Moreover, it was not until Abram moved his tent and settled in the dwelling place of someone named Mamre, who was an Amorite that lived in the city of Hebron, that he was called Abram the Hebrew, because he lived in Hebron with Mamre the Amorite. As it says in *Genesis 13:18*: "And Abram moved his tent, and came to dwell at the terebinths of Mamre, [which are in Hebron]; and he built an alter there to the LORD." *Genesis 14:13*: "A fugitive brought the news to Abram the Hebrew, who was dwelling at the terebinths of Mamre the Amorite, kinsman of Eshkol the Aner, these being Abram's allies."

"The Bible says that when Abram became ninety-nine years old, the LORD appeared to Abram and made an everlasting covenant with him. The scripture says that this covenant was called the "faith" covenant, and it consisted of two parts. The first part of this covenant concerned Abram's natural side, which consisted of both Abram and his wife Sarai, their son Isaac, Isaac's son Jacob, and the rulers or kings that would descend from his natural children. The reason God did this was to establish a natural race or nation on earth after His own name, whereby He could reveal Himself and His laws and commandments to humanity, as well as to have a nation that would fulfill all of His major prophecies, which concerned the entire world, even those prophecies that have not yet been fulfilled. Then ultimately, to bring about His plan of salvation, which would be in the person of Jesus Christ, who was of their offspring. So that everyone on earth out of every nation or ethnicity that would live by faith in God and accept Jesus Christ as Gods way of redemption, could then be grafted into this "faith" covenant through Jesus Christ, and thereby be able to bless themselves by the covenant that was made with Abraham. As it says in *Genesis 12:2-3*: "I will make of you a great nation, and I will bless you; I will make your name great, and you shall be a blessing. I will bless those who bless you and curse him that curses you; and [all the families of the earth shall bless themselves by you]."

The second part of this covenant consists of the new names that God gave to Abram and to his entire family that would forever associate them as the fathers of this faith covenant, so that everyone on earth who lives by faith in God just as they did would also have the right to call them their fathers. Therefore, God changed Abram's name from Abram to Abraham, which means the father of a multitude of nations. His wife Sarai's name was changed from Sarai to Sarah, which means the mother of many nations; and because God already named Isaac before he was born with a spiritual or eternal name that would forever associate him with this covenant, he is automatically given the same title under this covenant as his father Abraham. Finally, God also reaffirmed His covenant with Isaac's son Jacob when He changed his name from Jacob to Israel, which means the father of an assembly of nations as well. As it says in *Genesis 17:3-5, 15-16, 19*: "Abram threw himself on his face; and God spoke to him further, 'As for Me, this is *My covenant* with you: [you shall be the father of a multitude of nations]. And you shall no longer be called Abram, but your name shall be *Abraham*, for I make you the father of a multitude of nations.' And God said to Abraham, 'As for your wife Sarai, you shall not call her Sarai, but her name shall be *Sarah*. I will bless her; indeed, I will give you a son by her. I will bless her so that she shall give rise to *nations*; rulers of peoples shall issue from her.' God said, 'nevertheless, Sarah your wife shall bear you a son, and you shall name him *Isaac*; and [I will maintain My covenant with him] as an everlasting covenant for his offspring to come.' *Genesis 35:9-12*: God appeared again to Jacob on his arrival from Paddan-aram, and He blessed him. God said to him, 'You whose name is Jacob, you shall be called Jacob no more, but *Israel* shall be your name.' Thus He named him Israel. And God said to him, 'I am El Shaddai. Be fertile and increase; [a nation], yea [an assembly of nations], shall descend from you. [Kings shall issue from your loins]. The land that I assigned to Abraham and Isaac I assign to you; and to your offspring to come will I assign the land."

2. What is the Real name of God's children, Christian or Israel?

As I mentioned in question one of this chapter, if you have faith in the God of Abraham, Isaac, and Israel, and you believe that Jesus Christ is the one whom God sent into the world to redeem you back to Himself. Then you are a part of His covenant of faith with

Abraham, and that makes you a child of God. But the question is, what should you call yourself, a Christian or an Israeli?

The Bible says that anyone who was not naturally related to Abraham was often referred to as a Gentile, which in 1 Thessalonians 4:5 and Ephesians 2:11-22 literally means someone from another nation who is either not a part of the family of God or is "without" God in the world and does not know Him. In addition, because there were many Gentiles coming to the Lord in the New Testament, the Gentiles decided to refer to themselves as Christians in Acts 11:26, because they felt that they had no right to call themselves Israelis. However, as I mentioned in part one, the names Abraham, Isaac, and Israel are their spiritual or eternal titles that were given to them by God, and these names refer to them as the fathers of faith. This means that whether or not you are a Hebrew, if you live by faith and you believe that Jesus Christ is the Messiah, then under the covenant of faith your true forefathers are Abraham, Isaac, and Israel, and you are an Israeli. On the other hand, whether or not you are a Hebrew, if you do not live by faith and you do not believe that Jesus Christ is the Messiah, then you do not have any right to call them your forefathers, because they are the forefathers of those who live *by faith*. Because the covenant of *faith* was not made under their carnal or natural side and names, it was made under their spiritual side and titles.

Here are a few examples where you will find this coming from the LORD Himself through His Holy Spirit. Starting in *Exodus 12:15*: "Seven days you shall eat unleavened bread; on the very first day you shall remove leaven from your houses, for *whoever* eats leavened bread from the first day to the seventh day, [that person shall be cut off from Israel].'

You may have noticed that it did not say that this particular person would be killed, but rather this person would be cut off from having any rights to the name of Israel and all things that pertain to that name, whether they are naturally related to Israel or not, by saying "whoever." Another good example is in John 8:31-40, when God through His Holy Spirit spoke through the mouth of Jesus Christ to the Jews who believed on him and said. "If you continue in my word, then you will be my disciples indeed; and you shall know the truth (in other words you shall know me, and I will make you

ANCIENT MYSTERIES OF THE BIBLE REVEALED

free)." Then they said to him, "We are Abraham's children, and we were never in bondage to any man: how can you say that we shall be free?" Then Jesus said to them, "Truly, truly, I say to you, whoever committeth sin. In other words, whoever committeth sin because he abides or lives in sin is the servant of it. And the servant or the sinner that lives in sin abides not in the house forever: but the Son abides forever, and if the Son makes you free, then you are free indeed." Then because God promised Abraham that He would never again call him Abram, because of the everlasting covenant that God made with "Abraham." Jesus could not say to them that he knew that they were Abram's children, so he more or less said. "I know that you are Abraham's children, but you seek to kill me, because my word has no place in you. Then he said to them, I speak what I have seen done with my Father: and you do the things that you have seen done with your father." Then they said to him, "Abraham is our father." Then Jesus plainly said to them that the man that they know from God's covenant as "Abraham" was not their father, by saying to them (the Jews). If you were "Abraham's" children, you would do the works. In other words, you would live by *faith* and do the *things* that *Abraham* did. Then he went on to say to them, "But you seek to kill me, a man who has told you the truth which came from God: this did not "Abraham." Therefore, in other words, you must not be his children, because "Abraham" did not act like you, as it says here in *John 8:31-40*:

Then said Jesus to those Jews which believed on him, if ye continue in my word, then are ye my disciples indeed; and ye shall know the truth, and the truth shall make you free. They answered him, we be Abraham's seed, and were never in bondage to any man: how sayest thou, ye shall be free? Jesus answered them, verily, verily, I say unto you; whosoever committeth sin is the servant of sin. And the servant abideth not in the house forever: but the Son abideth ever. If the Son therefore shall make you free, ye shall be free indeed. I know that you are Abraham's seed; but ye seek to kill me, because my word hath no place in you. I speak that which I have seen with my Father: and ye do that which ye have seen with your father. They answered and said unto him, Abraham is our father. Jesus saith unto them, if ye were "Abraham's" children, ye would do the "works" of "Abraham." But now ye seek to kill me, a man that hath told you the truth, which I have heard of God: this did not "Abraham."

Another example can be found in Isaiah 66:22 and Zechariah 2:15, where the Bible says that after God creates the new heaven and the new earth, the name of God's children under the covenant of faith from every nation on earth will not be Christian, but Israel. Because it's an everlasting name that will endure forever and it's an everlasting name that all of God's children will go by under the covenant. As it says in *Isaiah 66:22*: "For as the new heaven and the new earth which I will make shall endure by My will — declares the LORD — so shall your seed and (your name endure)." *Zechariah 2:15*: "*In that day* many nations will attach themselves to the LORD and become His people, and I will dwell in your midst. Then you will know that I was sent to you by the LORD of Hosts."

Besides this, the apostle Paul in Romans 9:6-8 also tells us that just because someone is a natural descendent of Jacob doesn't mean he's a descendent of Israel. Likewise, just because they are the natural descendents of Abraham does not mean they are really "Abraham's" children. Because it says that Abraham's children will be called or named in Isaac. And he says that the natural descendents of Abraham are not the children of God, but those who live by faith in God as "Abraham" did are counted as his true descendents as it says in *Romans 9:6-8:* Not as though the word of God hath taken none effect. (For they are not all Israel, which are of Israel): Neither, because they are the seed of Abraham, are they all children: but, (IN ISAAC SHALL THY SEED BE CALLED). That is, (they which are the children of the flesh, these are not the children of God): but (the children of the promise are counted for the seed). Abraham's children were indeed called (named) in Isaac, and the name that was given to "Abraham's" children was Israel.

Beyond that, there is also another place in the Bible where Jesus himself says that *through* him [Jesus Christ] God's chosen people, Hebrew or not, will be called under one name, and that is Israel, and they will have one shepherd, which is Jesus Christ. This is what's referred to in Matthew 10:6 when Jesus said to his disciples "go to the lost *sheep* of the *house* of [Israel] ..." which in this verse means the natural descendents of Jacob. Then he says to them in John 10:14-16, and 24-26, that he has "other sheep" which are not of "this fold." In other words, other sheep which are not naturally related to Israel, that he must also bring, so that there shall be *one* fold of sheep and *one* shepherd. Then he goes on to say to the Jews that did not believe his words that they are not his sheep or his people. Then this implies as I mentioned earlier that the name of Israel does not belong to the natural descendents of Jacob who do not live by faith, but that the name of Israel belongs to all of God's children, Hebrew or not, who would live by faith in God as "Israel" did.

Therefore, under the covenant of faith, whether you are a Hebrew or not, Israel is your real eternal name. (Just keep in mind that when God addresses a nation directly, He always refers to them by the name of their nation.)

3. What is a saint? And what does someone have to do to become one?

The word saint means someone who is holy, faithful, or divine. It often refers to the angels who are already referred to as holy or divine, as well as human beings who have been called, devoted, or consecrated to the Lord to become saints. In other words, everyone who has been called to be holy, faithful, or divine through the blood of Jesus Christ and his salvation.

In Daniel 8:13 of the King James Version, you will find the word saint used three times to refer to angels, but because of verse 14, there are some who might say that the word saint that is used three times in verse 13 refers to people, because the King James Version says in verse 14, "And he said unto [me]," which actually looks like its referring to Daniel, and thereby the other saints in verse 13 must be referring to humans. However, in the Tanakh (the Jewish bible), this is what you will see, starting in *Daniel 8:13-14*: Then I heard a [holy being] speaking, and another [holy being] said to whomever it was who was speaking, "How long will [what was seen in] the vision last-the regular offering be forsaken because of transgression;

the sanctuary be surrendered and the [heavenly] host be trampled?" He answered [him], "For twenty-three hundred evenings and mornings; then the sanctuary shall be cleansed."

Psalm 89:6: "Your wonders, O LORD, are praised by the heavens, your faithfulness, too, in [the assembly of holy beings]." *Job 5:1*: "Call now! Will anyone answer you? To whom among the holy beings will you turn?"

Now when it comes to human saints, this is what the Bible says concerning all of us who are called to be saints. Meaning holy, faithful, or divine through the blood of Jesus Christ and his salvation, starting with 1 Corinthians 1:2: "Unto the church of God which is at Corinth, to them that are [sanctified] in Christ Jesus, [called] to be saints, with all that in every place call upon the name of Jesus Christ our Lord, both theirs and ours."

Ephesians 5:3: But fornication, and all uncleanness, or covetousness, let it not be once named among you, as [becometh saints].

1 Samuel 2:9: He guards the steps of His [faithful], but the wicked perish in darkness-for not by strength shall man prevail.

Psalm 16:3-4: As to the [holy and mighty ones that are in the land], my whole desire concerning [them] is that those who espouse another [god] may have many sorrows!

Psalm 82:1-7: God stands in the divine assembly; among the divine beings He pronounces judgment. How long will you judge perversely, showing favor to the wicked? Judge the wretched and the orphan, vindicate the lowly and the poor, rescue the wretched and the needy; save them from the hand of the wicked. They neither know nor understand, they go about in darkness; all the foundations of the earth totter. [I had taken you for *divine beings*, sons of the most high, all of you]; but you shall die as men do, fall like any prince."

Chapter 6

Heaven: The Tabernacle of God

ᘓᓓᓎᘗ

1. How many heavens are there? Where is the Real Heaven? And what are the different names for Heaven?

Basically there are three heavens described in 2 Corinthians 12:1-4. The first heaven is the first atmosphere that we call the sky; the second heaven is the celestial area that we call the universe; and the third Heaven is just beyond the edge of the universe and is separated from the universe by an area of space that the Bible refers to as *night*, which is completely separate from the universe and the third Heaven and hides its view from the natural eyes of man, which I will discuss more about in question two of this section. It is the third Heaven that the Bible refers to as the tabernacle or dwelling place of God; it is also called paradise or the New Jerusalem.

However, when God first made the earth, the Bible says there were only two heavens. The first heaven (the sky), and what we now call the third Heaven (God's Kingdom). In Genesis 1:6-8 the Bible says that the earth was like a huge greenhouse, with water on the earth as well as water covering the entire planet above the sky, separating the sky from the area called night and God's Kingdom. In Genesis 1:14, the Bible says that the sun, moon, and stars, which are now in the second heaven, were originally placed in the first. Many scientists believe that our universe is expanding and stretching, and

85

that our sun is bigger than what it was before. This tells us that the second heaven itself was originally part of the first heaven. This can be compared to stretching a piece of fabric so much that it becomes either lighter or darker in color. As you will notice when you look up into the sky, the closer it is to the earth, the lighter it is in color, and the further it is from the earth, the darker it is in color. It tends to start as a light blue, then a little darker blue, and then as you look out into the universe, the colors change to a very dark blue to black. This tells us that before the stretching took place, the sun, moon, and stars was indeed closer, very much closer in fact, like the Bible says starting with Genesis 1:6-8: God said, "Let there be an expanse in the midst of the water, that it may separate water *from* water." God made the expanse, and it separated the water which was [below] the expanse from the water which was [above] the expanse. And it was so. God called the expanse [sky]. And there was evening and there was morning, a second day.

Genesis 1:14-19: God said, "Let there be [lights in] the expanse of the *sky* to separate day from night; they shall serve as signs for the set times — the days and the years; and they shall serve as lights in the expanse of the sky to shine upon the earth." And it was so. God made the two great lights, the greater light to dominate the day and the lesser light to dominate the night along with the stars. And [God set them in the expanse of the sky to shine upon the earth], to dominate the day and the night, and to separate light from darkness. And God saw that this was good. And there was evening and there was morning, a fourth day.

There are many different names for God's dwelling place in the Bible, which we call Heaven. But here's a few of them from the Old Testament as well as the New: "The Heavenly Mount Sion or Zion," "The Heavenly Mount Paran," "Teman," "Zaphon," or "Bizzaron," all of which means Heaven, "The Mount of assembly," "The LORD Is There," "The Holy or The New Jerusalem," "The bosom of Abraham," "Paradise," and "The bride of Christ" or "The bride of the Lamb."

2. How did God create heaven and earth? And what is the difference between the light and darkness in Genesis 1:1-5, and the lights of the sun, moon, and stars in Genesis 1:14?

The Bible says that God created heaven and earth through His Word, His first-born Holy Spirit, who came out of Him before the world was created, who later became a human being in the person of Jesus Christ (John 8:42, John 16:27, John 17:5 and 8, Colossians 1:15, and Hebrews 11:3). He can also be seen in Genesis 1:2 hovering over the surface of the waters.

Concerning the light that God refers to as [day], according to the theories of Albert Einstein, everything in life, whether it's invisible or tangible, is made out of electro-magnetic waves of light or what's also referred to as *light* itself. In his theory, he suggested that in order to produce invisible and tangible matter (in non-technical language, "things") there must be electro-magnetism to hold everything together. If you consider that everything in life consists of things that are being held together by electro-magnetic waves of light or just what we know as *light* itself, then this explains why God makes everything else after chapter 1:3 *through* His Word, His first-born Holy Spirit, who we now know as Jesus Christ.

When it comes to the darkness that God refers to as [night], many scientists say that at the edge of the universe or at its peak there is something called dark matter, an area of space that is filled with thick darkness that has not yet been truly discovered, having properties that are exactly the opposite of light. This darkness is what I truly believe to be the [night] referred to in Genesis 1:2-5. The Bible also says that between this area of darkness and the universe there is a point called [the extreme], that was at one time on the surface of the waters that covered the sky in Genesis 1:6-7, where our universe [now] meets this area of dark matter where light and darkness meet as described in Job 26:10. He drew a boundary on the surface of the waters at [the extreme] where light and darkness meets.

There is, however, the question that arises concerning the water that is referred to as "the deep" in verse 2 before God said to the Spirit of Christ, "Let there be light." I believe that the water which the Spirit of Christ swept over in Genesis 1:2, and the water that God used for the entire earth in verses 6-10, was the water of life that comes from underneath His throne. And I believe that the water we now have on the earth, which came from the water of life, lost its ability to give and sustain life after the fall of man, because its ability to sustain life did not come from the water itself but from God. For the Bible says in the future, when God places His Kingdom on the earth, after He renews the heaven and earth in Revelation 21:1. The heaven and earth will be purified and all the oceans or seas will be dried up and gone, except for one, the Dead Sea; the Bible says it will be cleansed by the water of life, which will flow right into it to take its place that will come directly from His throne inside the Temple in Ezekiel 47:1-12. Therefore, it would only have been in His nature to have done this in the very beginning as well.

Now, that being said, here is what the Bible reveals to us concerning what actually occurred before and during the creation of heaven and earth based on what God looks like (as previously discussed in chapter 1, questions one and two) and who Jesus Christ really is as His first-born Holy Spirit.

First, there was God, a Spirit being of immense everlasting fire who has no beginning or end. Then, proceeding out from underneath His blue sapphire throne came forth the water of life, sparkling like crystal, which He used to form a massive ball of water about the size of the earth. At this time, surrounding this ball of water (the deep), was the darkness that is referred to as [night], which blocks the view of God's Kingdom as I mentioned in question one of this chapter, covering its entire form. Then, proceeding out from God came forth His first-born Son (His first Holy Spirit), who then proceeds towards the water of life and starts to hover over its surface in Genesis 1:2. At this time, God then speaks to him and directs him by saying, "Let there be light." At that moment, since every Holy Spirit is literally a piece of fire that comes out of God, capable of doing anything that God requires through the immense power of heat and energy that they are made of (as I mentioned in chapter three, question two). Light and heat began to shine forth out of him, filling the entire form of the water of life. From that light, he then began to separate the water into two different sections by forming the different atmospheres in the center of it, which make up the sky or the first heaven. With the clouds at the very top of the sky that was just formed by the warming and cooling of the air in order to hold the water above it (Genesis 1:6-8; Job 26:8). After this, God then commands him to bring out the dry land from the water that is below the sky. At that moment, because every Holy Spirit is made of fire, liquid sulfur began to pour out of him into the center of the water, gradually building up to the surface. As it dries, he then brings it out, thereby separating the water under the sky into one place and allowing the dry land to appear in Genesis 1:9 — thus creating heaven and earth.

3. What does Heaven look like?

The Bible says that Heaven is the tabernacle of God, and according to the Bible, the city of Heaven is shaped like a cube. Its walls measure approximately 18,000 cubits — or 12,000 furlongs — or roughly 27,000 feet in circumference, which makes it 6,750 feet high and wide on each side, as described in Ezekiel 48:35:

Its circumference [shall be] 18,000 [cubits]; and the name of the city from that day on shall be "The LORD Is There." *Revelation 21:16-17:* And the city lieth foursquare, and the length is as large as the breadth: and he measured the city with the reed, [twelve thousand furlongs]. The length and the breadth and the height of it are equal. Moreover, when it comes to its thickness, the walls themselves are approximately two hundred and sixteen-feet thick or one hundred and forty-four cubits on each side. The Bible describes the city itself, as well as its streets, to be pure gold, like transparent glass with a golden hue. Therefore, it would be very difficult to distinguish the many different sections of the city, including the inner court and the outer court, as well as the Temple. Which brings up an interesting question you may have asked yourself: why does it say in Revelation 7:15, 11:19, 14:17, and 15:5-6, that there is a Temple in Heaven, but in chapter 21:22 John said that he saw no temple therein? Let's consider this for a moment: if one of the elders in Revelation 7:15 had already told John that there is a Temple in Heaven, it would be very difficult to see, which explains why John said, "I saw no temple therein.." Keep in mind that the entire city, as well as its streets, is made out of [transparent] gold. But if you want to know what the inside of the city looks like, just remember that everything God commanded the children of Israel to design on earth is similar to the way it is in Heaven. So if you go to Israel and visit Jerusalem, and you see towns or homes in the city, just remember what Jesus said in the gospel of *John 14:2-3:* "In my Father's house are many mansions: if it were not so, I would have told you. I go to prepare a place for you. And if I go and prepare a place for you, I will come again, and receive you unto myself: that where I am, there ye may be also."

Now, when it comes to the wall that surrounds the city, there are many who believe that the entire wall is transparent jasper and that the twelve foundations spoken of in Revelation 21:19-20 are placed directly underneath the wall as its foundations stones. However, the Bible says that the wall itself is designed like a stone or brick layered wall, but instead of mortar, it has transparent jasper as its mortar. Instead of stones or bricks it has twelve transparent precious stones or gems that are smooth like carbuncles, or what is now referred to as a cabochon, throughout the entire wall from top to bottom, and is also described as "The wall of gems," as it says here in *Isaiah 54:11-12*: "Unhappy, storm-tossed one, uncomforted! I will lay [carbuncles as your building stones] and make your foundations of sapphires. I will make your battlements of rubies, your gates of precious stones, "the whole encircling wall of gems." Also, because John in Revelation 21:19 said that each stone looked like a foundation, then most likely each stone would be either square or rectangular in shape with the names of the twelve apostles inscribed therein (see Revelation 21:14).

In addition, on each side of the wall there are three gates, each made out of a single pearl, having twelve gates in total, with an angel standing in attendance at each one. Moreover, engraved upon the gates are the names of the twelve tribes of Israel (Revelation 21:12 and 21). We are given a full description of the gates in *Ezekiel 48:30-34*: And these are the exits from the city: On its northern side, measuring 4,500 cubits, the gates of the city shall be — three gates on the north — named for the tribes of Israel: the Reuben gate, the Judah gate, and the Levi gate: one. On the eastern side, [measuring] 4,500 cubits-there shall be three gates: the Joseph gate, the Benjamin gate, and the Dan gate: one. On the southern side, measuring 4,500 cubits, there shall be three gates: the Simeon gate, the Issachar gate, and the Zebulon gate: one. And on the western side, [measuring] 4,500 cubits-there shall be three gates: the Gad gate, the Asher gate, and the Naphtali gate: one.

Besides its design, we are also given a glimpse of what it will be like when we see it from afar in *Isaiah 2:2*: "In the days to come, the Mount of the LORD'S House shall stand firm above the mountains and tower above the hills; and [all the nations shall gaze on it with joy]."

In Ezekiel 47:1-12, the Bible gives us an even more accurate description of the city of Heaven and how life will be like when God places His Kingdom on the earth. It even tells us more about the Temple of God and what direction it will face, and how the water of life that flows out of the Throne of God will flow out of the Temple and out of the city and become a stream that will spread to the eastern region. It describes how deep the water will become and how there will be places to fish, because the water of life will produce many fish like the fishes of the Great Sea and the locations of the trees of life, as it says here in *Ezekiel 47:1-12*:

He led me back to the entrance of the Temple, and I found that water was issuing from below the platform of the Temple-eastward, since the Temple faced east — but the water was running out at the south of the altar, under the south wall of the Temple. Then he led me out by way of the northern gate and led me around to the outside of the outer gate that faces in the direction of the east; and I found that water was gushing from [under] the south wall. As the man went on eastward with a measuring line in his hand, he measured off a thousand cubits and led me across the water; the water was ankle deep. Then he measured off another thousand and led me across the water; the water was knee deep. He measured off a further thousand and led me across the water; the water was up to the waist. When

ANCIENT MYSTERIES OF THE BIBLE REVEALED

he measured yet another thousand, it was a stream I could not cross; for the water had swollen into a stream that could not be crossed except by swimming. Do you see, O mortal? He said to me; and he led me back to the bank of the stream. As I came back, I saw trees in great profusion on both banks of the stream. "This water," he told me, "runs out to the eastern region, and flows into the Arabah; and when it comes into the sea, into the Dead Sea, the water will become wholesome. Every living creature that swarms will be able to live wherever this river goes; the fish will be very abundant once these waters have reached there. It will be wholesome, and everything will live wherever this stream goes. Fishermen shall stand beside it all the way from En-gedi to En-eglaim; it shall be a place for drying nets; and the fish will be of various kinds [and] most plentiful, like the fish of the Great Sea. But its swamps and marshes shall not become wholesome; they will serve to [supply] salt. All kinds of trees for food will grow up on both banks of the stream. [Their leaves will not whither nor their fruit fail]; [they will yield new fruit every month], because the water for them flows from the Temple. [Their fruit will serve for food and their leaves for healing]."

Now, compare this with *Revelation 22:1-2*: And he showed me a pure river of water of life, clear as crystal, proceeding out of the throne of God and of the Lamb. In the midst of the street of it, and on either side of the river, was there the tree of life, [which bare twelve manner of fruits], and [yielded her fruit every month]: and [the leaves of the tree were for the healing of the nations].

Chapter 7

The Lake of Fire: Eternal Chastisement

∽o∾

1. What is the difference between hell and the lake of fire? Where are hell and the lake of fire located? And why did God choose fire as an eternal punishment?

The difference between hell and the lake of fire is that they're both physical places, but hell is mainly a [spiritual prison of darkness], because it is comprised of caverns that are filled with the thick dark smoke that rises from the burning magma flowing inside the earth's outer core and mantle. The heat from the magma rises and escapes through crevices that lead into these caverns, and black smoke constantly builds up inside them. For this reason, because the smoke creates total darkness, making it virtually impossible to see anything at all, it is also referred to as the [Bottomless pit], Sheol, Hades, and Gehenna that Jesus said was located in the heart of the earth.

Moreover, just as the heart is not in the center of the chest but more to the left, the caverns of hell are closer to the earth's surface than its center. So close in fact that it is going to be opened in the distant future in the land of Edom by a small comet upon impact as described in Matthew 12:40 and Revelation 9:1-2. Hell was created by God as a temporary holding place for the spirits of the damned, as well as for the wicked angels who sinned against God by having intimate relationships with the daughters of humanity in Genesis 6:1-2 and 2 Peter 2:4. In addition, whoever ends up there will be tormented by [spiritual fire]; the tongues of fire are a metaphor of the human tongue, which symbolizes the emotions or feelings, as described in Luke 16:24 and James 3:6. The inhabitants of hell will feel like they're on fire, but it's not necessarily because of the heat of the smoke, but also from an emotional torment. We must remember that a spirit cannot feel [physical] pain, because spirits in hell do not have bodies, thus the agonizing emotional and spiritual torment.

Now, whereas hell is a physical prison of darkness for the spirits of the damned **inside** the earth, just underneath the land of Edom, the lake of fire is going to be a lake **on** earth that is filled with burning sulfur (lava), and those who end up there will have both their bodies as well as their spirits tormented. And we are told that the first two people to experience this eternal torment will be the Beast and his False Prophet, as it says here in *Revelation 19:20 and 20:10*: "And the Beast was taken, and with him the False Prophet that wrought miracles before him, with which he deceived them that had received the mark of the Beast, and them that worshipped his image. These both were cast "alive" [into a lake of fire burning with brimstone]. And the Devil that deceived them was cast into the lake of fire and brimstone, [where the Beast and the False prophet are], and shall be tormented day and night for ever and ever."

So when Jesus referred to hell as hell-fire in Mark 9:47-48 as being a place where a person will have "both" their soul as well as their body, and where their bodies will be filled with worms that will never die, what he was referring to was that someday God will merge hell with the lake of fire, which will contain the Beast, the False Prophet, and the Devil, and the two places shall become one and shall be known as hell-fire. He will accomplish this during a future event known as the great white throne of judgment, where He will resurrect the wicked back to life from hell and cast them, as well as hell itself, "alive" into the lake of fire by flooding the pit and caverns of hell (which already will have been opened in Revelation 9:1-2) with the burning sulfur of the lake of fire, as it says here in

Revelation 20:11 and 13-15: "And I saw a great white throne, and Him that sat on it, from whose face the earth and the heaven fled away; and there was found no place for them. And the sea gave up the dead which were in it; and death and [hell] delivered up the dead which were in them: and they were judged every man according to their works. And death and "hell" [were cast into the lake of fire]. This is the second death. And [whosoever] was not found written in the book of life was cast into the lake of fire."

The Bible not only says that hell and the lake of fire are both physical places, but it also describes them in detail. It says that in the future, after the lake of fire fills the pit and caverns of hell with burning sulfur, its exact and permanent location will be clearly visible to everyone in the land of Edom. In addition, there will be all sorts of animals and thorn bushes growing and living around the area, making their homes there. It also says that after God renews the heaven and the earth, the saints will travel outside, which I believe to be either outside of the Holy city or outside of the land of Israel. And they will look at the corpses of the people that are in the lake of fire, and the people shall be a horror to look at in the eyes of all flesh. As it says in *Isaiah 66:22-24*: "For as the new heaven and the new earth which I will make shall endure by My will — declares the LORD — so shall your seed and your name endure. And new moon after new moon, and Sabbath after Sabbath, all flesh shall come to worship Me — said the LORD. They shall [go out and gaze on the corpses of the men who rebelled against Me]: their worms shall not die, nor their fire be quenched; [they shall be a horror to all flesh]."

Isaiah 34:9-17: Edom's streams shall be turned to pitch and its soil to sulfur. Its [land] shall become burning pitch; night and day it shall never go out; its smoke shall rise for all time. Through the ages it shall lie in ruins; through the aeons none shall traverse it. Jackdaws and owls shall possess it; great owls and ravens shall dwell there. God shall plan chaos and emptiness for it. It shall be called, "No kingdom is there," [its nobles and all its lords shall be nothing]. Thorns shall grow up in its palaces, nettles and briers in its strongholds. It shall be a home of jackals, an abode of ostriches. Wildcats shall meet hyenas, goat-demons shall greet each other; There too the

Lilith shall repose and find herself a resting place. There the arrow-snake shall nest and lay eggs, and shall brood and hatch in its shade. There too the buzzards shall gather with one another. Search and read it in the scroll of the LORD: not one of these shall be absent, not one shall miss its fellow. For My mouth has spoken, it is His spirit that has assembled them, and it is He who apportioned it to them by lot, whose hand divided it for them with the line. They shall possess it for all time; they shall dwell there through the ages.

Considering that God is a being of everlasting fire and that we are His offspring, it would only make sense that God would use fire as a form of everlasting punishment to punish His lost children that have sinned against Him.

Chapter 8

Satan

᭜᭜

1. Who is Satan? What does he look like? And how did he fall from his position in Heaven?

When God began to create heaven and earth through His Word, the Bible says that on the fourth day of creation He created all the Heavenly creatures, including cherubs, and as their Spirits entered into their newly created bodies, they all shouted for joy in thanks to God as described in Job 38:7. There was one cherub in particular who was different from the others in that he was called the shielding cherub, because his role was to cover the entire area before the throne of God with brilliant colors of light emanating from the precious gems that were built into his wings, which were set in pure or transparent gold. As he walked up and down with his wings stretched out before the throne of God on the river of life that sparkles like crystal proceeding from the throne of God like a walkway. He would also walk among the seven Spirits of God as they hover before His throne, who are also known as the stones of fire, and as the light of God's robe would shine forth, it would pass through the gems in his wings to form brilliant beams of colorful light that would fill the area before the throne of God with beautiful colors. For this reason, this cherub was also referred to as the Shining One, the son of Dawn.

Now he is known as Satan, which means the adversary. The Bible says that shortly after he was created, he gained knowledge

ANCIENT MYSTERIES OF THE BIBLE REVEALED

and wisdom as he listened to God direct His Word, His first-born Holy Spirit, who we now refer to as Jesus Christ, on how to create heaven and earth, as I mentioned in chapter six, question two. Then just before the work of creation was completed, he became lifted up with pride because of his wisdom and beauty, and he felt that he could do a better job than God could, so he said within himself. "Because I know how God created heaven and earth, I will climb to the sky; [higher] than the stars of God I will set *my* throne. I will *match* the Most High."

When God heard those words, the cherub who once shielded the area before the throne of God with beautiful colors of light became God's adversary. Any creature that is physically and spiritually unclean and gets too close to God is devoured and struck down by the sulfur and lightning that automatically comes out of Him. Thus, the cherub who was once called the Son of the Dawn fell to the earth like lightning, and because the spirit of Jesus Christ was the first Holy Spirit to come out of God, this explains how Jesus could say what he said in *Luke 10:18*: "And he said unto them, I beheld Satan as lightning fall from heaven."

Isaiah 14:12-14: How are you fallen from heaven, O Shining One, son of Dawn! How are you felled to earth, O vanquisher of nations! Once you thought in your heart, "I will climb to the sky; [higher] than the stars of God I will set my throne. I will sit in the Mount of assembly, on the summit of Zaphon: I will mount the back of a cloud-I will match the Most High."

Ezekiel 28:11-17: The word of the LORD came to me: O mortal, intone a dirge over the king of Tyre and say to him: thus said the Lord God: you were the seal of perfection, [full of wisdom and flawless in beauty]. [You were in Eden, the garden of God; every precious stone was your adornment]: Carnelian, chrysolite, and amethyst; beryl, lapis lazuli, and jasper; sapphire, turquoise, and emerald; and gold beautifully wrought for you, mined for you, prepared the day you were created. I created you as a cherub with outstretched shielding wings; and you resided on God's holy mountain; [you walked among the stones of fire]. You were blameless in your ways, from the day you were created until wrongdoing was found in you. By your far-flung commerce you were filled with lawlessness and you sinned. So I have struck you down from the mountain of God, and I have destroyed you, O shielding cherub, [from among the stones of fire]. You grew haughty because of your beauty, you debased your wisdom for the sake of your splendor; I have cast you to the ground, I have made you an object for kings to stare at.

2. What kind of power does Satan use against mankind? And where is he now?

Satan is very powerful in terms of his physical strength and his ability to influence the minds of others, but he cannot step over the boundaries that God has placed around him. Many people blame Satan for everything that goes wrong in the world, but the majority of things that go wrong in the world actually takes place because of the wrong decisions that we as human beings make using our own free will, but that free will can certainly be influenced by the thoughts that Satan and his demons put into our minds.

It has been said that when God wants to bless you, He influences someone else to do so by putting favor into their minds concerning you. In the same way, whenever Satan wants to destroy you, many times he will influence someone else, quite often someone very close to you, by putting evil thoughts into their minds concerning you, so that when they act upon those thoughts concerning you, it brings discord. Satan's first tactic is to steal your dreams, kill your dreams, and ultimately destroy you and your dreams, and he usually does this by influencing your thoughts or someone else's thoughts toward you, so that he can stop you from being blessed. For example, let's say you walk into a store to buy something and you ask the man behind the counter if he has something in stock, because you have noticed it isn't on the shelves anymore. A negative thought may come into his mind concerning you, and it could come from his own mind or from an outside source like Satan or his demons, and it could show itself as either prejudice, hatred, jealousy, and so forth. For that reason, let's say he does have what you want in stock, but because of his negative thoughts concerning you, he will not help you. Another example of this influence is when you are making a decision to do something, and you know that you are able to do it, but because of either your own negative thoughts that arise in your mind, which show themselves as doubts. Or alternatively, those that come to you from Satan or his demons that tell you, "You can't do it!" or "You will never make it!" and so on, you decide to listen to those thoughts by acting upon them, and that stops you from being blessed. Therefore, the only power that Satan is allowed to use against humanity is the power to influence our minds, because when it comes to his physical strength, there is no mortal alive who can withstand the physical power of an angel, much less that of a fallen cherub. The Bible says that Satan, who is a fallen cherub, and his demons, who are fallen angels, are eternal beings who can be tormented but can never die, and they also have powers like unto the angels of God, because that's who demons once were. For this reason, God knows that if He was to allow Satan and his demons the power to use their influence through their physical strength on humankind, in the same way that they influence the minds of people by putting evil thoughts into their heads. There would be no one on earth able to stop them from bringing worldwide havoc and misery on humanity, and many believers on earth would find it very difficult to serve the Lord, because it would be like someone coming into their homes every single day and trying to murder them.

However, in Ephesians 6:12 we are told that Satan uses his powers of mental influence mostly on the leaders of the world and those in high places or positions by putting evil thoughts into their minds, so that he can corrupt them and influence the decisions they make concerning the entire world, which is why we should always pray for our leaders (1 Timothy 2:1-2).

The Bible says that Satan roams the entire world every single day like a roaring lion looking and stalking for believers (and sometimes even non-believers because he knows of their potential to be saved), to pounce on or to devour by influencing their minds. He also goes back and forth to Heaven daily to present himself before the LORD, to give an account of where he has been, and to accuse the believers before God for acting upon the very thoughts that *he* placed into their minds.

Job 2:1-3: One day the divine beings presented themselves before the LORD. The Adversary came along with them to present himself before the LORD. The LORD said to the Adversary, "Where have you been?" The Adversary answered the LORD, "I have been roaming all over the earth." The LORD said to the Adversary, "Have you noticed My servant Job? There is no one like him on earth, a blameless and upright man who fears God and shuns evil. He still keeps his integrity; so you have incited Me against him to destroy him for no good reason."

1 Peter 5:8-9: Be sober, be vigilant; [because your adversary the devil, as a roaring lion, walketh about, seeking whom he may devour]. Whom resist stedfast in the faith, knowing that the same afflictions are accomplished in your brethren that are in the world.

Revelation 12:10: And I heard a loud voice saying in heaven, now is come salvation, and strength, and the Kingdom of our God, and the power of His Christ: for [the accuser of our brethren is cast down, which accused them before our God day and night].

3. Is there a difference between the man of sin and the Antichrist? What is the ethnicity of the Antichrist? And how is Satan involved?

There are similarities and differences between the man of sin and the Antichrist. Many theologians believe that the man of sin is the Antichrist, and he is, but he will not *become* the Antichrist until he dies by the sword of God and resurrected from the dead in Revelation 11:7. The Bible says that just before God returns to earth in the event known as the Day of the LORD, the Beast (the man of sin), who is going to make peace with Israel for seven years just before the LORD returns to earth, is going to be an Assyrian. Moreover, we are told that when God returns to earth, He will destroy the man of sin with the sword of fire that will come out His mouth (see 2 Thessalonians 2:8, Isaiah 31:8, Isaiah 66:16, Daniel 7:11, Psalms 97:3, and Revelation 13:14).

Then after he dies, his spirit will descend to the bottomless pit of darkness (also referred to as hell). He will be held there temporarily until God sends His two witnesses from Heaven to prophesy in sackcloth to the people of the nations of the world who will be

ANCIENT MYSTERIES OF THE BIBLE REVEALED

occupying the natural Jerusalem for forty-two months after having been left behind when God returns to earth in the event known as the Day of the LORD. Then after they are done prophesying, the spirit of the Beast will ascend out of the bottomless pit and will be resurrected back to life, where he will then make war with them, and shall overcome them, and kill them (Revelation 11:1-7). Then in Revelation 12:7-12 we are told that there will be war in heaven: Michael the archangel and his angels will fight against the dragon or Satan and his demons; then Satan and his demons will lose their place and position in the universe and will be banished to the earth. At this point Satan will be so angry that he lost his important and powerful position in the second heaven that he will set out to destroy all of those who were left behind when the LORD returned to earth, those who decided to keep the commandments of God and the testimony of Jesus Christ. Satan will do this by giving the first beast (the man of sin who was just resurrected from the dead) the authority and power to become the Antichrist who will control the entire world in order to force the saints into a position where they would have to deny Jesus Christ by worshiping the beast, his image, and to receive his mark. Only the true believers in Christ will be strong enough to reject the Antichrist, his image, and his mark, and for their resistance they will be beheaded as it is described in Revelation 12:17, Revelation 13:1-18, and Revelation 20:4.

Chapter 9

Angels, Cherubs, and Seraphs

ᶜᔆᵒᔆ

1. What are angels? How many different kinds are there? What do they look like? And how powerful are they?

Angels are powerful beings that are sent by God to speak on His behalf and to execute judgment for Him. For this reason they are also referred to as God's messengers, ministers, representatives, lords, which means someone of authority and someone to be respected, and heavenly saints, which means holy or divine beings, as I mentioned in chapter five, question three regarding saints, as well as in Matthew 4:11, 2 Kings 19:35, Jude 14-15, Zechariah 4:5, and Acts 10:3-4. Angels were created before man, along with all the other Heavenly beings, on the fourth day of creation (Job 38:7).

The Bible says that angels fall into two categories or ranks. The first rank of angels consists of Gabriel and all the other angels. The second rank consists of only one archangel (which means [ruler] angel), Michael, and he is considered to be the leader, captain, or prince of them all. He is the prince or ruler of the angels, meaning prince of the first rank, as well as the prince and representative of the nation of Israel (see Daniel 10:21, Daniel 12:1, Jude 9, Revelation 12:7). We can get an idea of his rank in *Daniel 10:13*: However, the prince of the Persian kingdom opposed me for twenty-one days;

now *Michael* [a prince of the first rank] has come to my aid after I was detained there with the kings of Persia.

The Bible says that angels were created in the image of God (as well as man), which is why according to many rabbis, when God said, "Let us make man in our image," the word "us" that God was actually referring to was Himself and the angels. Contrary to popular belief, they do not have wings. According to the Bible, from Genesis to Revelation, an angel's [basic] physical appearance is always that of a man wearing a white linen robe, because their white robes represent the righteousness of divine beings or saints (Acts 1:10, Daniel 10:18, and Revelation 19:8). Physically they can look so much like ordinary men that when Joshua was approached by one, he did not recognize him, as it says here concerning the archangel before he became known as Michael, in *Joshua 5:13-14*: Once, when Joshua was near Jericho, he looked up and saw [a man] standing before him, drawn sword in hand. Joshua went up to him and asked him, "Are you one of us or of our enemies?" He replied, "No, I am [captain] of the LORD's host. Now I have come!" Joshua threw himself face down to the ground, and prostrated himself, and said to him, "What does my lord command his servant?"

However, it is important to remember that the reason angels were sometimes unrecognizable to others in those days is that in the days of the apostles and in ancient times, almost everyone wore robes. For this reason, I believe that this made it easier for angels to intermingle with human saints without being recognized. As I mentioned earlier, the Bible says that an angel's [basic] physical appearance is always that of a man wearing a white linen robe, because their white robe is the only clue that reveals to others who they are and what they represent. Which is the righteousness of saints, which in turn represents the righteousness of God, and for angels to wear unholy clothing would be unimaginable.

Angels also have the ability to radiate tremendous light from their faces that shines like lightning or electricity, and this light makes them look so powerful and frightening that no one is able to look directly at them until they decide to let the light from their face diminish at will. An example of this is found in Matthew 28:1-4 and Mark 16:1-6, which when placed back to back, speaks of the same angel who came down from heaven and rolled the stone away from Christ's tomb, and his face is described as shining like lightning. This angel then stepped into the tomb and chose to diminish the light from his face at will, to disguise himself as an ordinary young man, just before Mary Magdalene and Mary the mother of James came to the sepulcher.

Besides having the power to radiate light as bright as lightning from their faces, we are told that when their full appearance of power is revealed, their faces shine as bright as lightning — they literally have fire for eyes. The brightness of their entire body shines as the beryl stone, and the skin of their arms and legs have the "color" of burnished bronze. When they speak, it is as if an entire multitude was speaking the same words at the same time through them, as it says here in *Daniel 10:5-6:* "I looked and saw [a man] dressed in linen, his loins girt in fine gold. His body was like beryl, his face had the appearance of lightning, his eyes were like flaming torches, his arms and legs had the "color" of burnished bronze, and the sound of his speech was like the noise of a multitude."

Angels also have the ability to dematerialize their bodies and literally transform themselves into any shape, even a pillar of fire, as in the case of one in particular who represented God fully, meaning not only representing Him physically as a pillar of fire, but also by literally bearing His name. The Bible says that the angel who appeared to Moses as fire in the burning bush at the foot of the mountain, who was also referred to as God in Exodus 3:2-4, and the angel who went before the children of Israel to lead them out of the land of Egypt as a pillar of fire by night and a cloud by day, hovering a few feet off the ground and was said to be the LORD that was looking down through it in Exodus 14:19-20, and 24; and the pillar of fire that hovered over the Ark of the Covenant and traveled with them throughout all their journeys in Exodus 40:34-38, was the same angel that the LORD commanded the children of Israel to fear, because not only did this angel represent the LORD by looking like a small version of Him physically, but he also bore His name, which is why this angel was referred to as the Lord God, as it says here in *Exodus 23:20-22:*

I am sending an angel before you [to guard you on the way and to bring you to the place that I have made ready]. Pay heed to him and obey him. Do not defy him, for he will not pardon your offenses, since [My Name is in him]; but if you obey him and do all that [I] say, I will be an enemy to your enemies and a foe to your foes.

This is the reason the Bible says in *Hebrews 1:7:* And of the [angels] he saith, WHO MAKETH HIS ANGELS SPIRITS, AND HIS MINISTERS [A FLAME OF FIRE].

The Bible also says that the reason God's [Name] was in this angel is because the first Holy Spirit of God, who is also known as the Word of God or Jesus Christ. Who in fact was the first Holy Spirit to come out of God before the world was created (John 8:42, John 16:27, John 17:5 and 8, and Colossians 1:15), as I mentioned in chapter four question one, who [represents] God, was with this angel throughout the whole time (Acts 7:38).

However, I must also point out that the Spirit of Jesus Christ who was with the angel that accompanied the Israelites throughout all their journeys is not to be confused with God Himself. Who according to the Bible is a being of fire that only revealed Himself [once] to Moses and the entire nation of Israel on the [top] of Mount Sinai as a massive fire with dark smoke covering the entire mountain. And with the underneath part of His blue sapphire throne sticking out of His fire as a pavement, as described in Exodus 19:9-24 and Exodus 24:9-11 and 16-17.

2. What are cherubs? How many are there? And what do they look like?

Cherubs are creatures that were created by God's Word to minister to God and accompany Him and His seven Spirits when He travels through the heavens, and next to each of them there is a wheel that is referred to as the wheelwork, and these wheels travel alongside them as they accompany God when He travels. These wheels receive their power to levitate and fly from the seven Spirits of God, who are also known as the spirits of the creatures, because they travel to and fro [among] them. According to the Bible, cherubs were created along

ANCIENT MYSTERIES OF THE BIBLE REVEALED

with all the other Heavenly creatures on the fourth day of creation (Job 38:7).

The Bible says there are four cherubs who remain with God now, but originally there were five. The fifth one stood before the throne of God with wings of gems stretched out and was known as the Shining One, the son of Dawn. Now, because of his sin against God, he is known as Satan or the adversary, as I mentioned in chapter eight, question one.

As for their physical appearance, as well as the wheels themselves, this is what the Bible says concerning the four cherubs in *Ezekiel 1:5-21*: In the center of it were also the figures of four creatures. And this was their appearance: they had the figures of human beings. However, each had four faces, and each of them had four wings; the legs of each were [fused into] a single rigid leg, and the feet of each were like a single calf's hoof; and their sparkle was like the luster of burnished bronze. They had human hands below their wings. The four of them had their faces and their wings on their four sides. Each one's wings touched those of the other. They did not turn when they moved; each could move in the direction of any of its faces. Each of them had a human face [at the front]; each of the four had the face of a lion on the right; each of the four had the face of an ox on the left; and each of the four had the face of an eagle [at the back]. Such were their faces. As for their wings, they were separated: above, each had two touching those of the others, while the other two covered its body. And each could move in the direction of any of its faces; they went wherever the spirit impelled them to go, without turning when they moved. Such then was the appearance of the creatures. With them was something that looked like [burning coals of fire]. This fire, suggestive of torches, kept moving about [among] the creatures; the fire had a radiance, and lightning issued from the fire. Dashing to and fro [among] the creatures was something that looked like flares.

As I gazed on the creatures, I saw one wheel on the ground next to each of the four-faced creatures. As for the appearance and structure of the wheels, they gleamed like beryl. All four had the same form; the appearance and structure of each was as of two wheels cutting through each other. And when they moved, each could move

ANCIENT MYSTERIES OF THE BIBLE REVEALED

in the direction of any of its four quarters; they did not veer when they moved. Their rims were tall and frightening, for the rims of all four were covered all over with eyes. And when the creatures moved forward, the wheels moved at their sides; and when the creatures were borne above the earth, the wheels were borne too. Wherever the spirit impelled them to go, they went-wherever the spirit impelled them-and the wheels were borne alongside them; for [the spirit of the creatures was "in" the wheels]. When those moved, these moved; and when those stood still, these stood still; and when those were borne above the earth, the wheels were borne alongside them-for the spirit of the creatures was in the wheels.

Ezekiel 10:12-13: Their entire bodies — backs, hands, and wings — and the wheels, the wheels of the four of them, were covered all over with [eyes]. It was these wheels that I had heard called "the wheelwork."

3. What are seraphs? How many are there? And what do they look like?

Seraphs are creatures that were created by God's Word along with all the other Heavenly creatures on the fourth day of creation (see Job 38:7). They were created to surround the throne of God in Heaven, to attend on Him, and to worship and praise Him without any rest, 24 hours a day, 7 days a week, for all eternity. The Bible says there are four of them. Their physical appearance is like that of cherubs, but instead of four wings they have six, and instead of four faces they have one, and instead of a single rigid leg they have two legs, as it says here in *Isaiah 6:2-3*: Seraphs stood in [attendance] on Him. Each of them had [six wings]: with two he covered his [face], with two he covered his [legs], and with two he would fly. And one would call to the other, "Holy, holy, holy! The LORD of Hosts! His presence fills all the earth!"

Revelation 4:6-8: And before the throne there was a sea of glass like unto crystal: and in the midst of the throne, and round about the throne, were four beasts full of eyes before and behind. And the first beast was like a lion, and the second beast like a calf, and the

ANCIENT MYSTERIES OF THE BIBLE REVEALED

third beast had a face as a man, and the fourth beast was like a flying eagle. And the four beasts had each of them [six wings] about him; and they were full of eyes within: and they [rest not day and night], saying, Holy, holy, holy, Lord God Almighty, which was, and is, and is to come.

Printed in the United States
85617LV00007B/79/A